UNDERSTANDING HOW OTHERS MISUNDERSTAND YOU

Workbook

Ken Voges & Ron Braund

MOODY PRESS

CHICAGO

All Scripture quotations, unless noted otherwise, are from the *New American Standard Bible,* © 1960, 1962, 1963, 1968, 1971, 1972, 1973, 1975, and 1977 by The Lockman Foundation, and are used by permission.

The copy of *Biblical Personal Profiles,* by Ken Voges, bound at the back of this workbook, was published initially by Performax Systems, International, Inc., Minneapolis, Minnesota, in association with In His Grace, Inc., Houston, Texas, © 1977 by John G. Geier, © 1985 Performax Systems International, Inc., and is used by permission of the Carlson Learning Company.

Tables 1 and 3 (adapted) are taken from *Understanding How Others Misunderstand You,* by Ken R. Voges and Ron L. Braund (Chicago: Moody, 1990), and are used by permission of The Moody Bible Institute of Chicago.

The following exercises and charts are either taken directly from or are adapted from material in Level 1:A, *Understanding Yourself and Others,* of The Biblical Behavioral Series, by Ken Voges (Minneapolis, Minn.: Performax Systems, International, Inc., 1986), and are used by permission of the Carlson Learning Company:

> The exercise in chapter 2, "Applying the Intensity Index to Peter" (adapted from section 3, "Scripture Characters and Personal Profiles," pp. 13-15, 26); the charts in chapters 5, 7, 9, and 11 that describe the basic skills of and the complementary skills needed by the classical profiles (adapted from similar charts on pp. 10-11); the "Classical Patterns" charts that appear in chapters 5, 7, 9, and 11 (taken from the charts on pp. 18-21).

The charts that appear in chapters 6, 8, 10, and 12 relating to work efficiency and personal compatibility of the classical profiles are adapted from similar charts appearing in Level 2, *The Job Factor Analysis System: Finding Your Place of Service,* of The Biblical Behavioral Series, by Ken Voges (Minneapolis, Minn.: Performax Systems International, Inc., 1986), p. 18, and are used by permission of the Carlson Learning Company.

Appendix A, "Classical Patterns and Scriptural Parallels," Appendix B, "Creating Loving Environments," and Appendix C, "Jesus' Personal Profile," are taken from material presented by Ken Voges in seminars throughout the country and are used by permission of In His Grace, Inc.

ISBN: 0-8024-1099-5

3   5   7   9   10   8   6   4

Printed in the United States of America

CONTENTS

About the Authors

Ken Voges (B.A.) is president of In His Grace, Inc., which provides believers and the church with behavioral tools and training. He is the author of the *Biblical Personal Profile,* an assessment tool that measures behavioral style and relates it to a positive biblical profile. Serving as field manager for PERFORMAX, Mr. Voges conducts training sessions for the *Biblical Personal Profile.*

Mr. Voges and his wife, Linda, are active in the Spring Branch Community Church in Houston, where he teaches an adult Sunday school class and is chairman of the elder board. They have two children, Randy and Christy.

Ron L. Braund (M.Ed., D.Min.), has served individuals and couples for more than twelve years as a licensed marriage and family therapist. Dr. Braund is a clinical member of the American Association for Marriage and Family Therapy (AAMFT) and directs an expanding network of Christian counseling centers in the Atlanta area. He has been instrumental in leading and developing the International Congress on Christian Counseling, a forum for the ongoing integration of theology and psychology among mental health professionals and pastors.

In addition to his clinical work, Dr. Braund is president of the Institute for Leadership Development (ILD), offering consultation and training to universities, corporations, and churches across America. ILD links successful leaders and organizations with a values-based approach to network business concepts.

Foreword

I first met Ken Voges when I was a pastor in Houston, Texas, in the mid-1970s. Early in our friendship I shared a few insights with him and his wife, Linda, concerning temperament differences and their effect on marriage relationships. Finding these ideas personally helpful, Ken soon began to pursue studies in the area with diligence and tenacity.

First reading on the subject of personality theory, then attempting to teach classes on the subject, then discovering the instruments developed by the Carlson Learning Company, then studying biblical biographies in depth with the help of able exegetes, and by repeatedly testing those conclusions in group settings and in personal counseling, then, after more than fifteen years of study and teaching, Ken and Dr. Ron Braund have produced a book and workbook that thoroughly correlate analyses of temperament types with data on biblical personalities.

Other books and resource materials have been on temperament differences, but this study is unique. The reader will be impressed with four major distinctives. First, the study is directly correlated with a well-respected instrument for measuring four key temperament traits. Second, Ken and Ron have presented a large number of biblical personalities from which the reader can find one similar to himself. Third, the focus of the book and workbook is directed toward the development of loving environments for others. And fourth, the pages are enriched with numerous personal examples.

Because Ken has been a great help to me personally over the years, and because Dr. Braund offers a valuable perspective as a licensed marriage and family therapist, I am especially excited over the publication of these volumes. They have provided insights helpful to me in my relationship with my family and in solving management problems that I have faced as a pastor and as a university president.

I commend the Voges and Braund book and workbook, *Understanding How Others Misunderstand You,* as both interesting and helpful personal reading and as a useful guide for group study, especially when used in conjunction with the *Biblical Personal Profile* instrument.

JOE L. WALL, TH.D.
President, Colorado Christian University

Preface

Some 15 years ago, I (Ken) was introduced to a behavioral model that identified different personality styles. It was extremely helpful to my wife Linda and me in understanding that differences are normal. Up until that time we were doing what many other married couples were practicing . . . trying to change our partner to be like us. It wasn't working.

These new concepts helped us accept one another as we began viewing differing styles as strengths rather than weaknesses. Shortly thereafter, I began teaching adult Sunday school classes, integrating some of this information into my presentations. The reactions were generally positive. Participants began to focus on personal needs and to accept personality differences as being normal. New levels of understanding developed for most. Unfortunately, for others greater insight created a potential for misuse. Some class members used the information as an excuse for their behavior and even labeled others with negative tags.

This development disturbed me because I knew the information had much positive potential, if presented properly. I felt the key to overcoming the problem had to be in using the Scriptures alongside the material. I began to analyze the behavior of personalities found in Scripture. That became a useful approach for helping others to associate their behavior with positive biblical models. The main focus of my teaching shifted to the Scriptures, which also helped overcome negative uses of the information.

In 1979, Betty Bowman introduced me to the Performax DiSC model of behavior. The Performax instrument, *The Personal Profile System,* allows a participant to personally analyze his behavior as a tool to increase his effectivenes with others. I spent the next five years testing these concepts against the unique behavioral styles of biblical characters. It was a fascinating study. The characters came alive from the pages of Scripture. After the associations were made, I began to work on a revision of the *Personal Profile System.* This effort culminated with Performax publishing what is now identified as the *Biblical Personal Profile.* Currently, over 100,000 instruments have been used with church groups, in counseling sessions, and for staff team building.

One afternoon in 1985 I (Ron) was talking with Bruce Edwards, the youth minister of a church our counseling organization serves in Atlanta, Georgia. He showed me a copy of the *Biblical Personal Profile.* As a licensed marriage and family therapist, I had used several assessment tools with clients in order to help understand their personalities. I had even developed a seminar using a temperament analysis as the foundation for improving communication. Upon exploring the *Biblical Profile,* I recognized it as a valuable tool for helping people to understand one another.

This version of the DiSC material gave insight into how others are motivated and into how misunderstanding tends to surface between people. Relating different behavioral styles to personalities like Peter, Paul, Moses, and Abraham provided powerful metaphors for integrating biblical truth with psychological principles.

Not long after beginning to use these instruments I became a managing consultant with the Carlson Learning Company. They publish the Performax instruments, including the *Biblical Profile.* After requesting more information on the *Biblical Profile* material, I was encouraged to call Ken Voges in Houston, Texas. Ken invited me to meet with him, and several weeks later I flew to Houston and received training from Ken and his lovely wife, Linda. Out of that experience, a close working relationship developed. Since that time, I have traveled throughout the United States training others to use the *Biblical Profile* and have been involved in developing additional material along with Ken. We have different behavioral styles and have had the opportunity to apply the truths contained in this book.

Our study of this material has revealed that the God of the Bible is far more personal than we had ever realized. He clearly understands the needs of each one of us and modeled the way to understand and love one another rather than to react and reject one another. The purpose of this workbook—and the book that accompanies it—is to help you understand how others may be misunderstanding you and to help you relate your unique behavioral style to a positive biblical character. This discovery can reinforce in your thinking the truth that God has a special purpose for your life. In addition, our desire is that you will be able to devise specific love strategies for improving the quality of relationships with your partner, your children, your friends, and your associates. Your reward will be to experience personal fulfillment and to become more effective in serving Christ.

CHAPTER 1
RECOGNIZING DIFFERENCES

Assignment:
Understanding How Others Misunderstand You,
chapter 1, pp. 15-31

The purpose of this session is twofold: to introduce ways to recognize differences in personality styles among people and to discover your own personality style by taking the *Biblical Personal Profiles* instrument. The workbook and the textbook that accompanies it are based on the idea that God gave each of us a unique cluster of behavioral characteristics. Those behavioral characteristics include a set of distinct needs. When we recognize what our own needs are we will be better able to understand—and meet—the needs of others.

Unfortunately, personality differences often become barriers to accepting one other and living out the biblical command to show unconditional love. Identifying and understanding diversity among personality profiles is a big step in learning how to cooperate with others instead of struggling with ineffective communication.

9

What Makes Us Different?

We often assume that others think the way we do. But they don't. Similarly, we often assume that we know what accounts for the differences we do notice. But we don't. Respond to the first set of questions below individually. Then share your answers with your partner or, if you are completing this workbook as part of a seminar, with the other members of your discussion group.

When you have completed your discussion, move on to the second set of questions. As you do, think about the differences in personality the questions reveal.

On the answer blanks indicate your agreement or disagreement with the following statements. Then discuss your reasons for making the choices you did.

1. Men have different expectations for personal relationships than do women.

   _____

   _____

2. Women have different emotions than do men. _____

   _____

3. Individuals who are committed Christians will have fewer conflicts in their

   personal relationship than those who are not. _____

   _____

4. People who yield in conflicts demonstrate Christian love. _____

   _____

5. A woman who finds it necessary to clarify her needs to her husband and tell
   him how to meet those needs is married to a man who is insensitive and lacking

   in perception. _____

   _____

Choose one of the following by underlining your preference.

1. Do you see yourself as being more **outgoing** or **reserved**?
2. If you see yourself as **outgoing**
   do you see yourself as being more of a **director** of others or as a **relator** to others?
3. If you see yourself as **reserved**
   do you see yourself as being more **accepting** or **assessing** of others?
4. When you are under pressure, do you tend to **express your thoughts** or to **keep them to yourself**?
5. As you approach a job, is it your preference to **communicate** with people or to **complete** an assigned task?

Differences in Perception

Differences in behavioral style among people are related to more fundamental differences in perception, motivation, needs, and values. **Look at the drawing of the glass and place a check mark beside the response at the right that best matches your description of it.**

_____ The glass is half full.

_____ The glass is half empty.

_____ The glass is either half full or half empty.

_____ I really don't care.

Some people see the glass in terms of fullness and some see it in terms of emptiness, but strickly speaking, all four responses are accurate. For what is being asked for in this instance is a person's initial response to the glass. All four responses can be normal within a group. In fact, the danger to the personality lies in denying people the right to an honest, candid reaction to what they see.

This difference among people in what they see when they look at the glass is a difference of _perception._ It is one of the factors that make up a person's unique personality style.

Differences in Motivation

When it comes to understanding motivation, it is important to distinguish between **how** a person is motivated and the **environment** he needs for that motivation to occur. The following statements explain general principles related to motivation.

1. You cannot motivate other people.
2. However, all people are motivated.
3. People usually do things for their reasons, not your reasons.
4. The very best one can do to motivate others is to create an environment that allows individuals to motivate themselves.

What motivates you might not motivate someone else. The questions below will help you begin to discover the environment you need if you are to be truly motivated.

Describe what is motivating for you:

_____

_____

Describe what discourages you from being motivated:

_____

_____

Differences in Needs and Values

Clarifying the differences between our needs-motivated behavior and our values-motivated behavior further identifies the way each person understands himself and others.

Needs-motivated Behavior	Values-motivated Behavior
What is most natural for us	What others and/or we expect of us
The "would do's" of living	The "should do's" of living
What is most pleasurable	What is right
What we feel is easiest	What we think is best
What is most practical	What is most meaningful

Needs-motivated behavior has to do with the behavior that is easiest and most natural for us. It is the type of behavior dealt with in the DiSC system used in this workbook and the accompanying text. Values-motivated behavior has to do with what we think is right, reasonable, and meaningful, and what we believe others expect from us.

Identify the following situations as involving needs- or values-motivated conflict. Place an _N_ on the line for a needs-motivated conflict and a _V_ on the line for a values-motivated conflict.

1. A person fails to meet a deadline on a project despite a genuine effort to complete it. _____
2. A Christian education director changes his Sunday school attendance report to the pastor in order to reach the church's published high attendance goal.

   _____
3. A manager with an organized and goal-oriented mind has difficulty meeting the same standards he demands from others. _____
4. A colleague promises to support your position in a job dispute but sides with the boss, who expresses the need for a different course of action. _____

Why We Need to Learn About Needs-motivated Behavior

Learning about needs-motivated behavior is necessary to better meet the needs of others and in turn fulfill Christ's commandment in Matthew 22:34-39 (italics added):

> Hearing that Jesus had silenced the Sadducees, the Pharisees got together. One of them, an expert in the law, tested him with this question: "Teacher, which is the great commandment in the Law?" Jesus replied: " *'Love the Lord your God with all your heart and with all your soul and with all your mind.'* This is the first and greatest commandment. And the second is like it: *'Love your neighbor as yourself.'* " All the Law and the Prophets hang on these two commandments.

Jesus' response, which quoted Deuteronomy 6:5 and Leviticus 19:18, emphasized a personal relationship with God as being the most important (v. 37), and the relationship between ourselves and anyone who comes into our area of influence (v. 39) as being the next in importance. The word Jesus used for love was *agapao,* which refers to a level of love that is both self-sacrificing and attached to meeting the needs of others. Jesus' position was that if you practiced these two commands, all other laws would be fulfilled.

Christ's second commandment, "Love your neighbor as yourself," expresses a great truth about human relationships. If you sacrifice yourself without taking care of your own needs, you will have nothing of quality left to give to others. The only way we can ever love others in a self-sacrificial way is by first having a clear understanding of ourselves and how to take care of our own needs (physical, emotional, and spiritual). When we have a grasp of those needs we will be capable of serving the needs of others.

The DiSC model used in this workbook and the accompanying textbook is a tool you can use to get a better idea of what your own needs are and how they can best be met. It will also help you understand the needs of others and what you can do to meet their needs.

> "You shall love your neighbor as yourself"
> means
> meeting others' needs
> in concert with meeting your own needs

Summing it up: The DiSC model measures _____ and is intended to be used as a tool to help you fulfill Christ's command.

Differences Are by God's Design

God designed our differences. Respond to the questions below as a means of confirming God's involvement in shaping your unique behavioral style.

1. Look up Psalm 139:1-3, 13-14. What does the psalmist communicate concerning your unique personality style?

   _____

   _____

2. Look up Galatians 1:15-16. What does the apostle Paul indicate God had prepared for him to accomplish from his birth?

   _____

   _____

3. Is your personality similar to or different from that of your father, mother, brother(s), and sister(s)?

   _____

   _____

Identifying Your Personality Profile

The purpose of this part of the session is for you and a partner of your choosing to take the *Biblical Personal Profile* so that you can identify your unique personality style. The *Biblical Personal Profile* can be given to you in a class or seminar by an administrator or you can take it by yourself. In either case, read the information below before you complete the Profile.

What the *Biblical Personal Profile Offers You*

Misunderstandings about what the *Biblical Personal Profile* offers can keep you from getting full value from it. The following paragraphs will give you important information about the goals of the *Profile* and the way it is organized.

1. The *Biblical Personal Profile* is a learning tool and not a clinical test. You cannot pass or fail this instrument. The most consistent results will be achieved by being open and accurate in your responses.
2. There are no good or bad "profiles." Each personality profile gives tendencies that identify specific strengths and weaknesses in each behavioral style.
3. The *Profile* only describes normal behavior. The emphasis is on identifying your individual potential rather than on identifying pathology.
4. The *Profile* portrays behavioral tendencies. Although it draws predictive conclusions, it is primarily designed to help you become more aware of your own and others' traits.

5. Try to make instinctive responses rather than responding the way you might think a "good Christian" should answer. You are measuring behavioral tendencies and skills that are needed in the Body of Christ. Your personality style will be matched with a biblical character God used to accomplish His purpose on earth.

Specific Instructions

The *Biblical Personal Profile* is bound at the back of this workbook. Detach it from the workbook now and return to these instructions.

Taking the *Profile* involves completing four steps:

1. Selecting the "Focus" you will use as the basis for your responses on the "assessment" page of the *Profile* (p. 2).
2. Completing the assessment page.
3. Tallying your responses.
4. Preparing the DiSC graphs.

Note that the **assessment** page (p. 2), the **instructions** (pp. 3-4), the **tally box** page (p. 5), and the **Intensity Index** page (p. 8) *are repeated* so that a partner of your choosing can take the instrument also.

Step 1: Selecting the "focus."

1. Turn to page 3 of the *Profile.* You will notice that you are asked to select the "focus" you will be using in filling in the assessment page of the profile.
2. This "focus" is a setting in which you function with other people. You may choose one of the following specific settings:
   a. *Work* focus: If you are interested in describing yourself in your work environment, the resulting interpretation will describe your behavioral tendencies in the work setting.
   b. *Personal* focus: If you are interested in describing yourself in a setting that relates to specific personal relationships, the interpretation will describe your behavioral tendencies in that environment.

   If this is the first time you have taken the *Biblical Personal Profile,* the authors suggest that you focus on your tendencies in the work environment. Homemakers might focus on their social environment outside the home.

Step 2: Completing the assessment (response) page (p. 2).

1. On the assessment page are 24 blocks in which are written descriptive words and phrases. In each block there is a "most" column and a "least" column.
2. Work box by box, making the selections you believe are appropriate. For each box, do the "most" column first, selecting the word or phrase that is *most* descriptive of you. Then do the "least"

column, selecting the word or phrase that is *least* descriptive of you.

3. It should take you about 7 to 9 minutes to complete the *Profile*. **Research reveals that the best results are obtained by giving your initial response.** You might expect some internal struggle over making your selection. This, too, is normal for most of us.

Step 3: Tallying your responses.

1. Turn to page 3 of the *Profile* and remove the perforated covering to reveal the tally box.
2. Follow the directions for **counting and recording** your results and for **determining the difference** between the most and least columns on the assessments page. To determine the difference in column 3 of the tally box, subtract column 2 from column 1.

Step 4: Preparing the DiSC graphs.

1. Turn to page 4 of the *Profile* and follow the instructions for plotting the three graphs.
2. Use the numbers in the **most** column of the tally box to plot Graph I on page 5 of the *Profile*.
3. Use the numbers from the **least** column to plot Graph II.
4. Use the numbers from the difference column to plot Graph III. If a specific number is not listed in Graph III, plot your graph between the numbers listed.

Step 5: Determining your *"segment numbers"* for page 5.

1. Turn to page 9 of the *Profile* and follow the instructions for completing the four-digit segment number. Example: 3-2-5-6.
2. Turn back to page 5 of the *Profile* and record your segment numbers below each graph.

Step 6: Determining your *"Classical Patterns"* for page 5.

1. Turn to the graph reference tables found on pages 9 through 12 that match segment numbers with Classical Patterns.
2. Locate your specific segment numbers and Classical Patterns. Record the pattern under each segment number on page 5 of your *Profile*.

Step 7. Determining your *"Biblical Model"* for page 5.

1. Turn to page 20 to find the **DiSC Classical Patterns** and **Positive Biblical Model** parallels.
2. Locate and underline your specific patterns for Graphs, I, II, III. Record the appropriate biblical names on page 5 of the *Profile*.

INTERPRETING THE BIBLICAL PERSONAL PROFILE

Assignment:

Understanding How Others Misunderstand You,
chapter 2, pp. 33-52

Now that you have taken, scored, and plotted the graphs in the *Biblical Profile,* you are ready to begin your interpretation of the *Profile.* While you review your *Profile* results keep in mind the following principles:

1. There are no better or bad profiles in this instrument.
2. You are what you are and you do not need to think that your profile requires major changes.
3. Each of us has individual strengths and areas in which we need to grow.
4. Successful people are those who
   - understand themselves and how they tend to affect other people
   - can identify their own strengths and weaknesses without being defensive
   - have developed the ability to be flexible and adjust their behavior style in order to meet the needs of a specific situation or to relate to people with different profiles.

Overview of the DiSC System

Table 1, DiSC Overview, identifies the distinctive characteristics of the four DiSC personality styles and shows how they are related to one another. It also shows how each personality style reacts to the different environments, what they are likely to emphasize in a given situation, and the goals they characteristically have.

DiSC Overview

focuses on
Changing the Environment

Dominant director
Goal: Authority & Action

Influencing relator
Goal: Persuasion & Motivation

emphasizes
Tasks &
Results

emphasizes
Ideas &
People

Compliant controller
Goal: Consistency & Standards

Steady supporter
Goal: Specialization & Cooperation

focuses on
Maintaining the Environment

TABLE 1

In the DiSC system the term *high* refers to the high points on the line graphs prepared for the Profile. Conversely, the term *low* refers to the low points on the line graphs. Thus a person whose high point is in the D column would be called a High D, whereas someone whose low point is in the D column would be described as a Low D. Table 2, High and Low DiSC Styles, describes the characteristic behavior traits of the four basic personality styles in terms of opposites, "high" and "low" styles placed side-by-side for contrast.

The general highlights on page 7 of the *Biblical Personal Profile* give a listing of the four dimensions of DiSC behavior. Turn to this page and reread the instructions for personalizing the tendencies that correlate with the highest points on your graphs.

High and Low DiSC Styles

	High Styles	Low Styles
D DOMINANCE	Tend to take an active, assertive, direct approach to obtain results.	Tend to obtain results by an organized, deliberate, indirect approach.
I INFLUENCING	Tend to approach new people in an outgoing, gregarious, socially aggressive manner. Tend to be impulsive, emotional, reactive.	Tend to approach new people in a controlled, sincere, reserved manner. Tend to place a premium on control of emotions. Make use of logic.
S STEADINESS	Tend to prefer a deliberate, predictable environment. Like secure situations. Value disciplined behavior.	Tend to prefer a flexibile dynamic, unstructured environment. The "Don't fence me in" types, who desire freedom of expression.
C COMPLIANCE	Tend to prefer that things are done the "correct way"— according to tested procedures and precise standards.	Tend to operate independently, believing "The right way is my way." Bottom-line oriented.

TABLE 2

Guidelines for Interpreting
the *Biblical Profile*

The purpose of the *Biblical Personal Profile* is to help you understand yourself and others. It features a self-interpreting process involving four stages. A detailed explanation of these stages is found on page 6 of the *Profile*. However, the brief explanation below of the four stages and how to proceed in the self-interpreting process will be helpful.

1. General highlights of the DiSC model (p. 7).
2. Intensity Index (p. 8)
3. Classical Patterns (p. 13-19)
4. DiSC Environments (p. 21)

Stage 1: General highlights (p. 7)
1. Circle your highest plotting point on Graphs I and II on page 5.
2. Turn to page 7 and focus on the DiSC square that corresponds to your highest plotting point(s). Underline the descriptive phrases that are accurate of you.
3. Mark through those phrases that do not describe you.

Stage 2: Intensity Index (p. 8)
1. Turn to page 8 and complete the assignments as outlined.
2. Respond to the highlighted words as they relate to your behavior.

Stage 3: Classical Patterns (pp. 13-19)
1. Turn to page 13 and read the explanation of the specific Classical Patterns and how they relate to your behavior.
2. Locate your specific patterns and underline those statements that are true of you.

Stage 4: DiSC Environments (p. 21)
1. Turn to page 21. Again, focus on the DiSC square that correlates with your highest plotting point in Graphs I and II. Review the statements under "**Remember, a High _____ May Want.**" Circle those statements that accurately describe what you want in a work setting.
2. Refocus on "**How to Respond to the High _____.**" Underline those statements that would help other individuals most effectively relate to you.

Applying the Intensity Index
to a Biblical Character

The intensity index was the means used to develop the Scripture parallels for the DiSC Classical Patterns. Turn to the next page of this workbook and complete the exercise.

WHERE DOES THE SCRIPTURE SPEAK ABOUT PERSONAL PROFILES?

Exercise: Applying the Intensity Index to the Apostle Peter

2 Timothy 3

16 All Scripture is inspired by God and profitable for teaching, for reproof, for correction, for training in righteousness,
17 that the man of God may be adequate, equipped for every good work.

Purpose:

This exercise will help you understand how to correlate the *Biblical Personal Profile*'s material with Scripture.

Scripture teaches us about God and the way He works in and through many different kinds of people. Peter was different from Paul. Moses was different from David. Mary was different from Martha.

Different as they were, God used each of these people. Notice, though, that He used them in different ways and in different places. What's more, He showed His divine love in different ways. Likewise, the Body of Christ is made up of different people.

To profile a Scripture character:

When you read a specific passage in Scripture

1. **Focus** initially on behavior.
2. **Faithfully accept** the recorded biblical account as accurate.
3. **Accept** the *Profile* Classical Patterns as credible.
4. **Study** the biblical character's tendencies and attempt to correlate his/her behavior with a Classical Pattern.

Peter:
A Behavioral Case Study

The Concept

Performax's profile information groups behavioral tendencies into fifteen specific, commonly identifiable Classical Patterns to explain why people respond as they do.

To find Peter's Classical Pattern, a quick word association using the Intensity Index on page 24 will be done to profile observed behavior.

The Assignment

1. **Read:** Matthew 14:22-33, focusing on the behavior of Peter.

2. **Underline the words:** In the scriptural amplification (exegesis) on the next page, underline words that reveal behavior.

3. **Locate word clusters:** Match Peter's behavior and the relevant terms on the DiSC Intensity Index for Peter (p. 24). On the Index, underline the behavior that matches Peter's. Look for word groupings (clusters) in each of the four scales (DiSC). By picking points near the center of the clusters for each DiSC column you should be able to develop a graph.

4. **Make your graph:** Transfer the cluster center points (as you see them) to Graph A on the next page. Use Graph B to record the profile discovered by the group you are working with. Note how close your graphs came to one another.

Matthew 14

22 And immediately He made the disciples get into the boat, and go ahead of Him to the other side, while He sent the multitudes away.

23 And after He had sent the multitudes away, He went up to the mountain by Himself to pray; and when it was evening, He was there alone.

24 But the boat was already many stadia away from the land, battered by the waves; for the wind was contrary.

25 And in the fourth watch of the night He came to them, walking on the sea.

26 And when the disciples saw Him walking on the sea, they were frightened, saying, "It is a ghost!" And they cried out for fear.

27 But immediately Jesus spoke to them, saying, "Take courage, it is I; do not be afraid."

28 And Peter answered Him and said, "Lord, if it is You, command me to come to You on the water."

29 And He said, "Come!" **And Peter got out of the boat, and walked on the water and came toward Jesus.**

30 But seeing the wind, he became afraid, and beginning to sink, he cried out, saying, "Lord, save me!"

31 And immediately Jesus reached out His hand and took hold of him, and said to him, "O you of little faith, why did you doubt?"

32 And when they got into the boat, the wind stopped.

33 And those who were in the boat worshiped Him, saying, "You are certainly God's Son!"

Scriptural Amplification

After the Lord fed five thousand people with five loaves and two fish, He sent His disciples across the sea in a boat, saying He would meet them on the other side.

In the middle of the night (3:00-6:00 A.M.), the disciples were still a long way from shore because the wind and waves were very strong against them, and Jesus came to them walking on the water.

The disciples were terrified, thinking Jesus was a spirit or a spectre, and they cried out in fear. The Lord calmed their fears immediately by calling out that it was Him. Peter responded by saying, "If it is you, command me to come to you on the water." Peter used a "first class" condition, indicating that in his mind there was no doubt it was really the Lord. Another translation might be, "Since you are out on the water, let me join you."

The Lord answered in the affirmative, "come," and Peter came, stepping out onto the water and walking toward Jesus. He was actually doing it because he wasn't worried about circumstances, only about the Lord. Then the impulse of the moment was over, and Peter realized what he was actually doing, saw the storm around him, became afraid (took his eyes off the Lord), and began to sink into the waves.

When Peter began to sink, he immediately cried out to Jesus for help. The tense of the verb he used literally implied, "Lord, save me, and do it quickly!" At that very moment Jesus reached out His hand, took hold of Peter, and said to him, "O you of little faith, why did you doubt?" The word Jesus used means "to be pulled two ways." What the Lord asked was, "Why, when you were being drawn to me in faith, did you allow yourself to be pulled back the other way?" (This was not a criticism of Peter's ability to display faith, but of Peter's inability to follow through with the faith with which he had begun as he stepped out of the boat.) Then they both got into the boat and the storm stopped.

Used by permission of Carlson Learning Company.

GRAPH A:

Place the graph you developed for Peter on this grid.

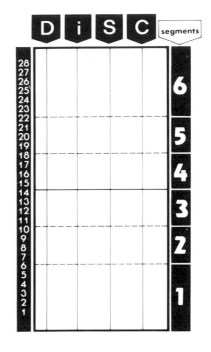

GRAPH B:

Place the graph your group developed for Peter on this grid.

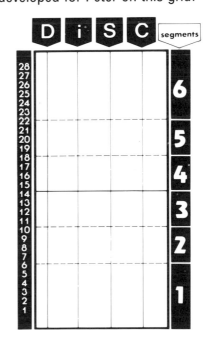

DiSC Intensity Index for Peter

	High D Dominance **Prefers to Be in Control**	High I Influencing **Prefers Involvement with People**	High S Steadiness **Prefers Predictable Structure**	High C Compliance **Prefers Procedures and Order**	
28 27 26 25 24 23	egocentric direct daring domineering demanding forceful	enthusiastic gregarious persuasive impulsive emotional self-promoting	passive patient loyal predictable team-person serene	perfectionist accurate fact-finder diplomatic systematic conventional	**6**
22 21 20 19	risk-taker adventuresome decisive inquisitive	trusting influential affable sociable	possessive complacent inactive relaxed	courteous conscientious restrained high standards	**5**
18 17 16 15	self-assured competitive quick self-reliant	generous poised charming confident	non-demonstrative deliberate amiable stable	analytical sensitive mature evasive	**4**
14 13 12 11	calc. risk-taker self-critical unassuming self-effacing	convincing effusive discriminating reflective	mobile outgoing alert eager	"own-person" self-righteous opinionated persistent	**3**
10 9 8 7	realistic weighs pros/cons unobtrusive conservative	factual logical controlled retiring	critical discontented fidgety impetuous	independent rigid firm stubborn	**2**
6 5 4 3 2 1	peaceful mild quiet unsure dependent modest	suspicious pessimistic aloof withdrawn self-conscious reticent	restless change oriented fault-finding spontaneous dislikes status quo active	arbitrary rebellious defiant obstinate tactless sarcastic	**1**
	Prefers to Be a Team-Player **Low D** Dominance	**Prefers to Be Alone** **Low I** Influencing	**Prefers Variety and Change** **Low S** Steadiness	**Prefers Spontaneous Approach** **Low C** Compliance	

Identifying Your Classical Pattern and Biblical Character

Research has shown that no more than 20 percent of the population is identified as having behavioral tendencies that are "pure" DiSC styles. For most of us, more than one DiSC trait significantly influences our personality make-up. The Classical Patterns in the *Biblical Personal Profile* offer a more precise level of interpretation. They identify fifteen of the most commonly occurring combinations of DiSC traits. The fifteen Classical Patterns describe behavioral tendencies in nine components.

Once you have identified your Classical Pattern, you can also select the biblical character of your choosing that the Scripture indicates closely resembles your unique behavioral style. Turn to page 20 of the *Profile* and look up the Bible verses listed there and compare your typical responses to the responses of the Bible characters.

DiSC Exercise

1. The classical Pattern I most relate to is the _____ because the following components are also true of me:

2. The biblical character I most identify with is _____ because:

A Look Ahead

Now that you have identified your unique personality style you are ready to begin learning how your tendencies compare and contrast with others. This discovery will help you see how misunderstandings often develop between people with different behavioral styles.

UNDERSTANDING EXPECTATIONS AND ENVIRONMENTS

Assignment:

Understanding How Others Misunderstand You,
chapter 3, pp. 53-68

DO YOU MEAN I MAY BE NORMAL ?

In order to build relationships, we must understand and respect differences as normal. Misunderstandings often occur when we think people should respond in ways consistent with our own natural responses. The purpose of this session is to identify how different expectations affect how we relate to one another.

Efforts to change rather than accept one another frequently lead to disagreements. The golden rule states, "Do unto others as you would like others to do unto you." This principle has helped guide us in treating our fellow man with more respect. One way to foster acceptance and minimize conflicts is to treat others the way we would like to be treated.

Identifying Expectations Exercises

A. Read the following and discuss the difference between the expectations of the two individuals.

Bill has agreed to meet Gene for a business lunch. Bill arrives ten minutes early in order to beat the crowd and get a table. He tells the waitress that he will order when his partner arrives. Now consider Bill's thoughts when it is fifteen minutes past the time Gene agreed to meet.

It has been twenty minutes, and Gene's late again. I don't think he has ever been on time. I should have known and been late myself, but I just can't do that. Now the waitress is annoyed at me because I have taken up a table too long. I feel embarassed—no, I feel angry. I bet Gene will have an excuse—he always does. Now he is thirty minutes late. Should I just leave? I can't believe he is so inconsiderate.

About this time, Gene drives up and rushes through the door. Listen to his thoughts.

Great. Bill hasn't left. I bet he's making good use of his time—he always does. That last phone call I got before leaving the office made me late, but it was very important. My customer was upset that he had not received his order, and I needed to smooth his feathers. Everything is fine now, and I even got the man to place another order for our new product line. Oh well, I have the rest of the afternoon free and can spend as much time as I need with Bill.

As Gene gets to the table, he says, "Hi, Bill. Sorry I am a little late. Things got busy at the office all of a sudden. Can we order now and then get down to business?"

We can see that Bill and Gene have a different perspective of what is important concerning being on time for the lunch appointment.

1. Which of the four DiSC profiles is most characteristic of Bill? What about Gene?

   _____

   _____

2. What were the different expectations of each man?

   _____

   _____

3. How could this problem be avoided on another occasion?

   _____

   _____

B. Suppose you agreed to a 12:00 P.M. luncheon with a friend. Look at the chart highlighting the expectations of the different DiSC styles. Describe what each profile would expect of himself and of you.

High C _____

High S _____

High D _____

High I _____

TABLE 3   Expectations

(The number 10 indicates high expectations, the number 0 low.)

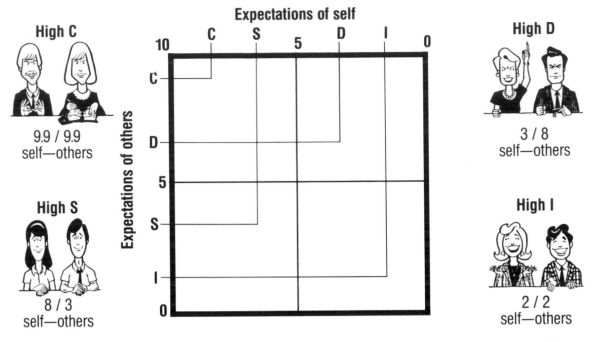

After studying the differences in expectations, return to page 27 and record what each DiSC profile would expect of himself and of you. (Relate these expectations to time, i.e., to 12:00 P.M.)

Understanding DiSC Environments

Behavior consultants have identified a modification of the golden rule. It is called the "platinum rule." The platinum rule is designed to increase our ability to relate to others. It states, "Do unto others the way they prefer to be done unto." In other words, if we learn how to treat others in a manner that is consistent with the environment within which they respond best, then we can move closer toward achieving harmony and understanding. Understanding DiSC environments involves developing our ability to respond to another person in a way that is consistent with his preferences.

Look at table 4, "DiSC Environments." If you followed the specific points outlined in this chart you will improve the quality of communication you have with others and minimize the chance of misunderstandings.

Apply the information contained in table 4 by working your way through the exercises on page 30, paying particular attention to the way you can "meet another person halfway" in your dealings with him by creating an environment in which he can flourish.

TABLE 4   DiSC Environments

HIGH D (PAUL) CASE STUDY: ACTS 9:3-19 *Remember, a High D May Want:* Authority, challenges, prestige, freedom, varied activities, difficult assignment, logical approach, opportunity for advancement.	HIGH I (PETER) CASE STUDY: JOHN 21:1-22 *Remember, a High I May Want:* Social recognition, popularity, people to talk to, freedom of speech, freedom from control and detail, recognition of abilities, opportunities to help and motivate others.
HOW TO RESPOND TO HIGH D'S Provide direct answers, be brief and to the point; confrontation may be necessary to gain their attention. Ask "what" questions, not how. Stick to business. Outline possibilities for the person to get results, solve problems, be in charge. Stress the logic of ideas or approaches. When in agreement agree with facts and ideas, not the person. If timelines or sanctions exist get them into open but relate them to end results or goal.	**HOW TO RESPOND TO HIGH I'S** Provide favorable friendly environment; never use confrontation if you want productive feedback. Allow them to express their intuition and ideas. Provide ideas for transferring talk to action. Provide testimonials of experts on ideas. Allow time for stimulating and fun activities. Provide details in writing but don't dwell on them. Create a democratic environment. Provide incentives for taking on tasks.
HIGH S (ABRAHAM) CASE STUDY: GENESIS 12-22 *Remember, a High S May Want:* Status quo, security of situation, time to adjust, appreciation, identification with group, work pattern, limited territory, areas of specialization.	HIGH C (MOSES) CASE STUDY: EXODUS 3-4 *Remember, a High C May Want:* Security, no sudden changes, personal attention, little responsibility, exact job descriptions, controlled work environment, status quo, reassurance, to be part of a group.
HOW TO RESPOND TO HIGH S'S Provide a sincere, personal, and agreeable environment. Show a sincere interest in the person. Ask "how" questions to get an opinion. Allow for and use visual illustrations. Be patient in drawing out their goals. Present ideas or departures from the status quo in a non-threatening manner; give them a chance to adjust. Define their roles or goals in the plan. Provide personal assurances of support. Emphasize how their actions will minimize their risk.	**HOW TO RESPOND TO HIGH C'S** Prepare your case in advance. Provide straight pros and cons of ideas. Support ideas with accurate data. Provide reassurances that no surprises will occur. Provide an exact job description with a precise explanation of how it fits into the big picture. Provide a step-by-step approach to a goal. If agreeing be specific. Disagreeing, disagree with the facts, not the person; strongly reject "poor-me" comments. Provide many explanations in a patient and persistent manner.

1. Let's suppose you were attempting to market a new product to a customer. While he talks with you on the phone he asks for many specific details and requests that you make a formal presentation. How would you prepare for that appointment?

_____

_____

_____

2. In your own words describe the major environmental differences of the:

   High D _____

   High I _____

   High S _____

   High C _____
3. Look up 1 Thessalonians 5:14. Which of the five words mentioned are most comforting to you when you are under stress: urge, admonish, encourage,

   help, patience? _____
4. Look again at the DiSC environments chart. Select the phrases in the chart that are most important for others to consider when they relate to you.

_____

_____

_____

_____

DiSC Communication Clues

Table 5, "DiSC Communication Clues," provides additional insight into what we can expect from the four DiSC personality styles. The chart identifies typical patterns of speech, writing, and listening.

A Look Ahead

Knowing what the DiSC personalities expect and the environments in which they flourish will give you a solid foundation for helping to resolve misunderstandings. Now we can look at everyday situations and anticipate what reactions to expect from the different DiSC styles.

TABLE 5

DiSC Communications Clues

	HIGH D	HIGH I	HIGH S	HIGH C
SPEECH PATTERNS	Direct, commanding speaker with focus on his own objectives in conversation. Will give commands rather than requests. Speaks rapidly. Usually in a hurry to communicate ideas.	Verbal, emotional speaker who personalizes his speech with his own adventures. Constantly seeks reactions from others to his comments.	Speaks slowly. Low keyed style. Speech often directed to concrete topics.	Tends to ask questions rather than make statements. Quiet and observes speaker. Very cautious about revealing any personal reactions.
WRITTEN COMMUNICATIONS	Short, sometimes incomplete communication. Prefers memos. Will write notes or letter and give to secretary to decipher. Will not usually thoroughly read correspondence.	Will have others write letters for him if possible. Prefers to telephone. Memos will have "happy face" or other drawing on them.	Will write clear, concise letters with excellent directions. Excellent at any written communication that follows lines of existing practices.	Best with written facts and figures. Will always have facts and in logical order. Written communications are precise and logical with no room for error.
LISTENING PATTERNS	Selective listener. Tends not to hear everything said to him. Does not like verbose explanations. Get to the point when speaking to this person.	Does not listen well. Prefers to do the talking. Tends to hear emotional tones in voices.	A natural listener who always tries to hear and understand the speaker. Will listen for ways he can help the speaker.	Will listen and assess everything the speaker says. Facial expressions will reveal nothing about his reactions. Will discard information of the speaker if any fact is incorrect.
WILL ASK	"WHAT" questions	"WHO" questions	"HOW" questions	"WHY" questions

THE DiSC PERSONALITY STYLES IN DAILY LIVING

Assignment:

Understanding How Others Misunderstand You,
chapter 4, pp. 69-77

We can better understand one another if we know what reactions to expect from the four DiSC personality styles in everyday life. If one picture is worth a thousand words, then a group of portraits will speak volumes. The claims of this proverb will come alive in this session as we use cartoons to help characterize our understanding of the differing ways each of us tends to respond to a similar set of circumstances.

Cartoons That Characterize Our Differences

An artist, Dan Dunn, has captured the distinctive qualities of the four DiSC personalities in a series of cartoons. These cartoons will give you a shorthand way of keeping in mind the distinct characteristics of the four DiSC personalities. That, in turn, will help you predict what you can expect from other persons. We ask that you not take the characterizations presented in the cartoons too personally. All of us need to loosen up and laugh at ourselves at the same time we are learning how to understand one another. We recommend that before you attempt to fit yourself into any one category, consider the fact that we all have a blending of several DiSC styles. Each of us is unique. The cartoons only highlight the extreme traits manifested by the personality styles.

Before you review the pictures of the various DiSC styles, there are some ground rules that have to be respected.

DiSC Ground Rules

Even though labels are a natural part of describing people, places, and things, inappropriate use of labels can be dangerous. If a label helps clarify differences, then it is useful. But if the label creates barriers, it can be harmful. At this point in your understanding of the DiSC descriptions, the following ground rules will help you exercise caution in applying the DiSC personality profiles to your daily life.

Ground Rules

Don't nudge

Don't pigeon-hole

Don't label others

Don't flaunt your knowledge

Don't use your knowledge as an excuse

Bible is final authority

Used by permission of In His Grace, Inc.

The High D (Dominant) cartoon is the one at the left. Notice that he has a more intense, non-nonsense look, as well as being more direct. The High I (Influencing) is at the top left center. This man is a bit more casual, with an outgoing look on his face indicating the tendency toward openness and friendliness. The High S (Steadiness) is at the right center. He has a more conservative look and is intent on being supportive. Finally, the High C (Compliant) is at the right. He is characterized as an intense thinker and someone who is more cautious and analytical. With these pictures in mind, let us look at the way these personality styles react to different situations in life.

The DiSC Personality Styles
in Daily Living

The four DiSC personality styles have characteristically different responses to various situations. Turn to chapter 4 in *Understanding How Others Misunderstand You* (pp. 69-77), and read the material in conjunction with the cartoons that appear on pages 34-40 of this workbook chapter.

Approach to Teamwork

High D: • initiates action
• takes charge
• moves out to reach a goal

High I: • draws upon contacts to gather the resources needed for the project

High S: • ensures follow through
• offers support

High C: • offers design, technical skills, and quality control

High D

High I

High S

High C

Leadership or Management Style

High D:
- adopts an autocratic style
- prefers hierarchy of leadership
- defines responsibilities
- implements actions
- manages trouble

High I:
- more democratic style
- facilitates open communication with and by others
- wants consensus to make the final decisions

High S:
- takes a participative role
- delegates daily decisions to others

supports by listening and allowing others to follow through on their assignments
- strives for peace and harmony

High C:
- leads with a more bureaucratic approach
- emphasizes proper procedures and completion of tasks
- desires compliance to procedures, but if they are followed allows individual initiative

High D

High I

High S

High C

Sensitivity to the Feelings of Others

High D:
- tends to be insensitive to the feelings of others
- sees emotional expressions as obstacles
- sees life as a battle

High I:
- is more sensitive to others
- wants others to be happy
- is quick to offer encouragement and reach out to others

High S:
- conscious of feelings
- tries to avoid hurting others
- avoids conflict and stirring up controversy

High C:
- task oriented
- takes a logical, analytical approach to feelings
- believes that what we feel about the way life is going for us is the consequence of the choices—good and bad—we have made

High D

High I

High S

High C

Releasing Stress

High D: • emotional intensity builds when personal goals are not met
• seeks a physical stress release
• prone to express fits of anger

High I: • under stress becomes more talkative
• releases nervous energy

physically but in a more emotional way than the High D

High S: • tends to internalize stress
• dislikes conflict
• releases stress by sleeping

High C: • prefers to tune out stress
• dislikes chaos
• wants to be alone at times of stress

High D

High I

High S

High C

Recovery from Emotional Stress

High D: • needs to get involved in a physical activity to recover from emotional stress

High I: • recovers from stress by spending time with others and by talking
• needs only a short time to recover from stress

High S: • needs sleep to recover from stress
• needs mindless "down time" to recover (watching television, working in the yard, taking a walk)

High C: • needs time alone
• reads a book or pursues a hobby as a way of recovering from emotional stress

High D

High I

High S

High C

Making a Spiritual Commitment to Christ

High D: • a traumatic event is needed to spur his recognition of a need for commitment to Christ

High I: • finds it easy to express his faith verbally and to make a public commitment to Christ
• looks forward to sharing his new experience with friends and family

High S: • surrenders to Christ with a minimum of attention being drawn to himself

• commitment is solid and sincere
• is tremendously loyal and gives years of faithful service to God

High C: • experiences internal struggle over whether he has done everything right
• battles with the issue of eternal security
• has a difficult time separating performance from God's grace

High D

High I

High S

High C

Being the Pastor of a Church

High D:
- wants the church to provide comprehensive programs for all people
- takes an aggressive goal-oriented approach

High I:
- is interested in programs that will reach an increasing number of people for Christ
- is emotionally expressive of his faith
- is good at eliciting passion for and participation in important causes

High S:
- prefers a traditional church
- wants to work toward peace and harmony
- stresses social services and community involvement

High C:
- wants the church to be operated "by the book"
- is cautious about new projects
- emphasizes doctrine and following proper procedures

High D

High I

High S

High C

DiSCovery Worksheet

In order to further discover the uniqueness of your profile, respond to each of the statements below.

1. When I looked at the cartoons I related best to the one that:

   _____

   _____

   _____

   _____

2. I would describe my leadership style to be:

   _____

   _____

   _____

   _____

3. I feel I have value to the team because I can:

   _____

   _____

   _____

   _____

4. I tend to handle stress by:

   _____

   _____

   _____

5. I recover from emotional stress by:

   _____

   _____

   _____

A Look Ahead

By now you should have a general understanding of what to expect from each one of the DiSC personality styles. The eight sessions that follow will take an in-depth look at each of the four main behavior patterns.

UNDERSTANDING THE DOMINANT STYLE

Assignment:

Understanding How Others Misunderstand You,
chapter 5, pp. 79-100

The **Dominant** or **High D** individual is direct, confident, and straightforward. The High D loves challenges, and it only inspires him to action when others caution, "It can't be done." High D's focus principally on goals and tasks. Frequently, the High D sees people only as a means to accomplish a goal. Whereas the High D and High C are likely to view events with an antagonistic focus, the High I and the High S are likely to focus on harmony and on creating a favorable, friendly environment.

We will focus in this lesson on how the Dominant styles work and how they relate to classical personality patterns in the other three profiles. In addition, we will discuss the ways the High D is likely to be misunderstood by others. Our goal will be to gain awareness of why conflicts with the Dominant personality style occur and what can be done to work through those issues to build solid relationships.

Finally, you will learn the basic tendencies of the four Classical Patterns in the High D family: **Developer**, **Results-oriented**, **Inspirational**, and **Creative**. We will also discuss the biblical characters that represent each of these High D patterns.

Understanding High D Tendencies and Skills

Basic Tendencies

1. High D's have a high sense of personal worth, or *high ego strength.*
2. High D's are *task-oriented* and *need results.*
3. High D's are motivated by *directness.*
4. The basic fear of the High D is that he will *be taken advantage of.*
5. The basic blind spot of the High D is that he *lacks concern for the feelings and views of others.*

Basic Skills

The High D possesses many dynamic skills. However, when a High D's tendencies are out of control, they can offend others by being too aggressive and by being insensitive to the feelings of others. To counterbalance those tendencies, a High D needs to have individuals around him who have skills that are complementary to his. Below are examples of various High D skills and the corresponding balancing skills in the other profiles. Notice that in the last column, the final three complementary profiles have been left out. Which profiles best represent the complementary skill?

Skills of the High D Profile	Complementary skills needed by the High D	Profiles who have the complementary skills
Tends to be	*Needs others who*	
Quick acting	Calculate risks	C
Decisive	Understand the whole picture	S
Practical	Are sensitive to other's emotions	I
Self-confident	Weigh the pros and cons	
Adept at solving problems	Act cautiously	
Independent	Recognize the needs of others	

Used by permission of Carlson Learning Company.

Understanding How the High D Relates to Others

The following compatibility chart identifies the natural manner in which a Dominant person generally relates to each DiSC behavioral style in personal relationships and in work settings.

Styles	Excellent 1 2	Good 3 4	Fair 5 6	Poor 7 8
D-D		P	W	
D-i		P	W	
D-S	W		P	
D-C			W	P

KEY

P = Personal Relationships

W = Work Tasks

1 = Best Possible

8 = Poorest Possible

Definitions—

D-D Team: High D's respect and admire others who are action-oriented. Consequently, they often carry a personal high regard for other High D's because both are committed to results. However, because of their high ego strength, D's frequently encounter difficulty in working together because they cannot agree on who should lead or follow in achieving mutual goals.

D-I Team: High I's have the relational skills that High D's need and admire. High I's are also action-oriented, which complements the High D's need for variety. The relationship between the two can become strained because the High D has a need to control, whereas the High I has a desire to be free of structure and control.

D-S Team: High D's work well with High S's because the D's generally provide the start-up energy, whereas the S's are committed to making sure the work is completed. High D's prefer leading, and High S's generally prefer following. The personal relationship between the two often suffers because High D's desire change and variety, whereas the High S's desire status quo.

D-C Team: The work relationship between the High D and the High C is difficult at times because the C is committed to maintaining structure and the status quo, whereas the D will interject change as a mode of operation. The personal relationship between the two suffers because the High D is direct and confrontational, whereas the High C is extremely sensitive to criticism and withdraws.

Misunderstanding the High D

Study the characteristics below and circle the traits that, in your opinion, could lead to misunderstandings.

Characteristics of the High D

1. *Dominant tendencies include:*
   solving problems
   causing action
   making quick decisions

2. *Desires an environment with:*
   power and authority
   activities that challenge the
     status quo
   brief and direct answers

3. *Judges others by:*
   ability to meet their standards

   aggressiveness
   quickness in accomplishing
     goals

Characteristics of the other DiSC styles

Tendencies of the other DiSC styles:
High I styles: entertaining people
High S styles: staying in one place
High C styles: concentrating on details

Desires an environment with:
High I styles: favorable working conditions
High S styles: security of the situation

High C styles: many patient explanations

Judges others by:
High I styles: verbal expression and
                    flexibility
High S styles: consistency and getting along
High C styles: commitment to precise
                    standards

Exploring exercise:

1. Study each of the 3 High D characteristics and compare them with the other DiSC styles. In your opinion, where do you feel major conflict would most likely occur?

   in the D/I combination:

   in the D/S combination:

   in the D/C combination:

2. In your opinion which combinations have the greatest potential for misunderstanding? Which have the least?

Understanding High D Classical Patterns

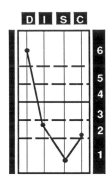

Developer

Solomon, Lydia*

1-EMOTIONS:	Very individualistic in meeting personal needs	Eccles. 2:1-11
2-VALUE TO THE ORGANIZATION:	New ideas; innovative problem solver; projects sense of power	1 Kings 3:16-28 Acts 16:13-15, 40
3-FEARS:	Loss of control	1 Kings 2:13-25
4-INCREASE EFFECTIVENESS WITH MORE:	Follow through and attention to importance of quality control	1 Kings 11:1-13

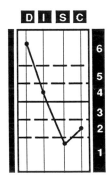

Results-oriented

Pharaoh (Exodus 5), Joshua, Sarah*

1-UNDER PRESSURE:	Becomes critical and fault finding	Genesis 16:4-6
2-INFLUENCES OTHERS BY:	Force of character	Joshua 24:1-16, 31
3-VALUE TO THE ORGANIZATION:	Takes charge; acts as catalyst to carry out difficult assignments	Joshua 1:1-18
4-FEARS:	Slowness especially in seeing a task or goal accomplished	Genesis 16:1-3

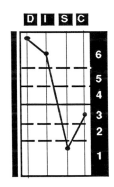

Inspirational

Laban, Apollos, Stephen

1-INFLUENCES OTHERS BY:	Charm, command of words	Acts 18:24-28
2-VALUE TO THE ORGANIZATION:	Skilled in verbal persuasion; can be intimidating	Acts 7
3-UNDER PRESSURE:	Control; rewards to get own way; can manipulate facts	Genesis 29:15-25 Genesis 29:26-30
4-GOAL:	Control his environment and those around him	Genesis 30:24-34 Genesis 30:19-55

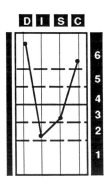

Creative

Paul, Michal*

1-EMOTIONS:	May be restrained in expression	2 Cor. 10:10; 11:5-6
2-INFLUENCES OTHERS BY:	Aggressively setting the pace in developing new systems	Gal. 1:15-16 Gal. 2:1-10
3-VALUE TO THE ORGANIZATION:	Creating change in making ''old systems'' better	Gal. 2:15-16 Acts 15:1-29
4-FEARS:	Others failing to measure up to his standards	Gal. 2:11-14 Acts 15:36-40

*Tendencies indicate a pattern, but not enough scriptural content to make a confident association.

High D Discovery Exercise

In your opinion, what tendencies make the High D unique?

How do the High D Classical Patterns differ from one another?

Developer

Results-oriented

Inspirational

Creative

High D's fear being taken advantage of and have a tendency to react forcefully when their territory is threatened. Read 1 Kings 2:12-25. What did Adonijah, Solomon's older brother, ask of Bathsheba? What did Bathsheba do?

If Solomon had granted his brother's request, Adonijah could have laid claim to the throne. How did Solomon react to his mother's request? How did he respond to his brother? How does this apply to High D behavior?

A Look Ahead

In the next lesson, we will look at what causes a High D to react to stress the way he does. In addition, we will suggest ways you can help the High D. Finally, we will study how Jesus dealt with the apostle Paul to help him grow in obedience and maturity.

RESPONDING TO THE NEEDS OF THE DOMINANT PERSONALITY

Assignment:
Understanding How Others Misunderstand You,
chapter 6, pp. 101-24

If you are to understand how to love a High D, you must first recognize what happens to him when certain of his needs are not met. As with the other profiles, a High D will protect himself in a predictable way. The High D needs an environment that offers difficult assignments along with the authority to confront the challenges of the tasks. When a High D profile senses outside pressures preventing him from achieving his personal goals, boiling internal energy begins to mount. Frequently, he will release this energy in an explosion of anger and/or punitive action directed toward those who block his goals.

In this session we will describe the situation that typically causes the High D to explode. In addition, we will look at a biblical case study in which a High D finds himself in a typical stress situation resulting in negative consequences.

Also, we will look at the elements necessary to give the High D the best opportunity to grow in a stressful situation. We will review a biblical case study showing how Jesus created a specific environment for the apostle Paul so that he had the opportunity to minister under God's authority and not his own. You will be given a chance to test the concepts discussed in this session through a series of questions designed for small group discussion.

Understanding High D Stress

Need issues: • Being in *control*
  • Accomplishing *personal goals*

The High D begins to encounter stress when

1. He has to submit to *authority* and thereby *lose control*
2. His personal goals are *blocked* or *threatened*
3. His common reaction is to *actively confront the person(s) creating the threat*
4. Their normal response will be to *confront back*
5. That results in *all-out confrontation—jungle warfare*
6. Communication deteriorates to a *messenger system*

Biblical Case Study: Exodus 5:1—6:11

Read the Scripture passage. What were the instructions Moses and Aaron communicated to Pharaoh, a High D? If God's plan were implemented, what effect would that have on Pharaoh's construction program—building monuments with his name on them? What was his response to Moses and Aaron, and what actions did he take to counter their plan? What was the response of Israel to Moses and Aaron? What did Moses and Aaron do? What was God's response? What D tendencies are present?

Understanding the High D Environment

1. High D's respond best to an environment that offers a *challenge,* but they sometimes need to be *confronted* in order to change the direction in which they are going.
2. When a High D's behavior is out of line, focus on his *action* and how he is *personally* affecting you.
3. Be *brief* and to the *point*—and then leave.
4. Following any confrontation, give him *time* to reflect before offering any more information.
5. Select a neutral *messenger* to give follow-up information.
6. Also, give *direct* answers and stick to business.

Assignment

If you know a High D, have him review the list above. Have the D pick at least one element that is important and meaningful in creating a loving environment for him. Record his response below.

Optional Exercise

To me, the most interesting element in dealing with the High D is:

Understanding Christ's style of loving Paul

Read Acts 9:1-22. In the left column, describe Christ's actions and/or Paul's reactions. In the right column, describe the environment that Jesus created as He spoke to Paul. How does Jesus' approach compare to the suggestions given on the previous page for loving the High D?

Christ's actions and Paul's reactions	The environment Jesus created
Acts 9:1-2 (Paul's actions)	Environment created by Paul
Acts 9:3-4 (Christ's actions)	Environment created by Jesus
Acts 9:5a (Paul's reaction)	
Acts 9:5b-6 (Christ's actions)	
Acts 9:7-8 (Paul's actions)	
Acts 9:9 (Paul's reactions)	
Acts 9:10-17 (Christ's actions)	
Acts 9:18-22 (Paul's reaction)	

Discovering the High D:
Worksheet for High D Profiles

This worksheet and the worksheet that immediately follows go together and should be discussed by specific groups. High D profiles should use this worksheet; Low D profiles (I's, S's, and C's) should use the worksheet on the next page.

After you have answered all the questions, share your answers with your partner, discussing your responses to question 1, then question 2, and so on. If you are using a discussion group method, select a spokesman to share the consensus of the group's findings. Then join the other three profiles for the group discussion.

1a. If I had to describe my behavior in three phrases, I would choose the following words

1b. I like jobs that have tasks which involve

1c. but would rather delegate tasks that involved

2. If I could select three key elements to incorporate into a loving environment for me, they would be

3. As I reflect on the environment Jesus created for Paul in Acts 9, I think He would also have ministered to me when He

4a. When I am under stress, the most loving thing you can do for me is

4b. I best deal with personal anger by

5. In order to develop better relationships with the other profiles, I continually need to work on the following areas of my behavioral style:

In relating to the High I

In relating to the High S

In relating to the High C

Loving the High D:
Worksheet for Low D Profiles

This worksheet is to be filled out by the Low D profiles (I's, S's, and C's) at the same time the High D's are filling out their worksheet. After you have answered all of the questions, share your answers. If you are using a discussion group method, divide into at least three groups (High I's, High S's, and High C's) and select a spokesman for each group. Rejoin the High D's and share the consensus of the group's findings, discussing one question at a time, alternating between the High D worksheet and the Low D worksheet.

1. The areas of my life where I need the gifts of the High D:

2. As I reflect on the environment the High D needs, the most difficult element for me to create and communicate is:

3. The one element Jesus used in Acts 9 in communicating with Paul that I would like to know how to use is:

4. As I review the differences in my style and that of the High D, I see the greatest *potential* for conflict to be:

    because

5. In order to build a better personal and working relationship with High D's, I need to be willing to modify my need to/for:

Bonus question:

6. If I were planning a date or other function with a High D, I would include the following activities:

55

CHAPTER 7
UNDERSTANDING THE INFLUENCING STYLE

Assignment:
Understanding How Others Misunderstand You,
chapter 7, pp. 125-42

The **Influencing** or **High I** individual is outgoing, persuasive, gregarious, and optimistic. He can usually see some good in any situation. He is principally interested in people, their problems, and their activities. High I's meet people easily and can be on a first-name basis with someone the first time they meet him.

In this session we will focus on how the Influencing styles work and relate to the other profiles. We will discuss how the High I's are likely to be misunderstood by others. The goal of this session is to gain awareness of why conflicts occur with the Influencing profiles and what can be done to build growing and solid relationships.

In this session, we will also discuss the basic tendencies of the High I and the family of Influencing Classical Patterns: **Promoter**, **Persuader**, **Counselor**, and **Appraiser**. We will also discuss the biblical characters that represent the four High I groups.

Understanding High I Tendencies and Skills

Basic Tendencies

1. High I's have a tendency *to be optimistic* and have a natural gift for *trusting* and *believing* in others by projecting unconditional acceptance.
2. High I's tend to be *socially-oriented* and are the most comfortable when they are relating to and interacting with people. They have the gift of reaching out to strangers.
3. High I's are motivated by *social recognition*.
4. The basic fear of the High I is *social rejection*.
5. Under pressure High I's can become *reckless* and *disorganized*.

Basic Skills

High I's have excellent social skills, but when a High I's tendencies are out of control, he is likely to compromise or to overlook critical commitments. To counterbalance those tendencies, the High I needs to have around him individuals who have complementary skills. Below are examples of various High I skills and the corresponding balancing skills in the other profiles. Notice that in the last column the final three complementary profiles have been left out. Which profiles do you think best represents the complementary skill?

Skills of the High I Profile	Complementary skills needed by the High I	Profiles who have the complementary skills
Tends to be	*Needs others who*	
Quick acting	Are self-disciplined	D
Initiator	Finish what has been started	S
Responsive	Develop systematic approaches	C
Compassionate	Can make unpopular decisions	
Joyous, upbeat	Act cautiously	
Optimistic, confident	Ponder information before acting	

Used by permission of Carlson Learning Company.

Understanding How the High I Relates to Others

The following compatibility chart identifies the natural manner in which an Influencing person generally relates to each DiSC behavioral style in personal relationships and in work settings.

Styles	Excellent 1 2	Good 3 4	Fair 5 6	Poor 7 8
I-D		P	W	
I-I	P			W
I-S	W		P	
I-C		W		P

KEY

P = Personal Relationships
W = Work Tasks

1 = Best Possible
8 = Poorest Possible

Definitions—

I-D Team: Because both High I's and High D's enjoy environments that include variety and change, they generally maintain good social relationships. However, when they begin to work together, their differences in focus can become a problem. High I's have a tendency to make decisions based on relationships, whereas High D's make decisions on the basis of cold facts and the bottom line.

I-I Team: High I's relate well to each other because they enjoy socializing and having fun together. However, their work ethic is poor because they enjoy talking so much. As a result, they seldom have time for work.

I-S Team: High I's work well with High S's because the I's have the verbal skills to sell the team's ideas, whereas the S's will commit to making sure the work is completed. Their personal relationship often suffers because High I's have a tendency to be inconsistent in their commitments and are constantly changing their plans, whereas the High S's desire stability and loyalty.

I-C Team: The work relationship between I and C is generally good because the I's need and depend on the C's ability to research the facts. Like the High S, the C's generally admire the I's ability to sell their ideas. Their personal relationship often suffers because the I's are free spirited and impulsive, whereas the C's desire structure and no surprises.

Misunderstanding the High i

Study the characteristics below and circle the traits that, in your opinion, could tend to lead to misunderstandings.

Characteristics of the High I

1. *Influencing tendencies include:*
   contacting people
   generating enthusiasm
   making a favorable impression

2. *Desires an environment with:*
   democratic relationships
   group activities outside of
      the job
   freedom from control and
      details

3. *Under pressure:*
   becomes soft and persuadable
   emotional, verbal and assertive

   can become manipulative

Characteristics of the other DiSC styles

Tendencies of the other DiSC styles:
High D styles: getting results
High S styles: calming excited people
High C styles: critical of performance

Desires an environment with:
High D styles: personal control
High S styles: minimal infringement on
                         home
High C styles: standard operating
                         procedures

Under pressure:
High D styles: confrontative and aggressive
High S styles: becomes quiet and
                         withdrawn
High C styles: becomes restrained and
                         sensitive to criticism

Exploring exercise:

1. Study each of the three High I combinations and compare them with the other DiSC styles. In your opinion, where do you feel major conflict is most likely to occur?

   in the I/D combination:

   in the I/S combination:

   in the I/C combination:

2. In your opinion which combinations have the greatest potential for misunderstanding? Which have the least?

Understanding High I Classical Patterns

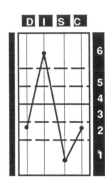

Promoter

Saul, Aaron

1-EMOTIONS:	High verbal skills; willing to accept others	Exodus 4:10-14 Exodus 4:27
2-OVERUSES:	Praise to gain approval	1 Samuel 15:1-31
3-VALUE TO THE ORGANIZATION:	Promotes people and projects	Exodus 4:28-31
4-UNDER PRESSURE:	Becomes careless and disorganized	1 Samuel 13:8-13
5-FEARS:	Loss of social recognition	Exodus 32:1-6

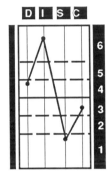

Persuader

Peter, Rebekah

1-EMOTIONS:	Trusts others; enjoys sponta-neity, change, and newness	Genesis 24:53-58
2-INFLUENCES OTHERS BY:	Reaching out to strangers	Genesis 24:12-38
3-VALUE TO THE ORGANIZATION:	Speaks with poise and confidence and has ''seller/closer'' skills	Acts 2:14-36 Acts 2:37-41
4-UNDER PRESSURE:	Becomes soft and persuadable when a social relationship is on the line	Acts 10:28 Galatians 2:11-12

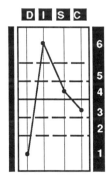

Counselor

Barnabas, Abigail

1-EMOTIONS:	Affectionate, encouraging	Acts 4:36-37 Acts 15:37-39
2-GOAL:	To gain harmony and happiness by persuading others with facts	1 Samuel 25:21-35
3-VALUE TO THE ORGANIZATION:	Practices an open door policy; understanding, good listener	Acts 9:26-27
4-OVERUSES:	Tolerance, indirect approach	1 Samuel 25:2, 3, 18, 19, 36-40

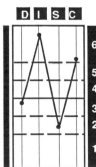

Appraiser

David, Miriam*

1-GOAL:	''Win'' with flair	1 Samuel 18:20-30
2-INFLUENCES OTHERS BY:	Competitive recognition; high drive to win	1 Samuel 16:18 1 Samuel 17:20–18:9
3-JUDGES OTHERS BY:	Use of charm and style in initiating activities	1 Samuel 25:2-42 (Note their styles/behavior)
4-UNDER PRESSURE:	Becomes restless like a coiled, quivering spring (Walking helps relieve tension.)	2 Samuel 11:1-27

*Tendencies indicate a pattern, but not enough scriptural content to make a confident association.

High I Discovery Exercise

In your opinion, what tendencies make the High I different from the High D?

What are some observable differences in the High I Classical Patterns?

Promoter

Persuader

Counselor

Appraiser

High I's fear the loss of *social recognition*. If they have to make a choice between maintaining a principle or a relationship, they will generally sacrifice their commitment to the principle.

Read 1 Samuel 15:1-31. What was Saul's assignment? What principles did he compromise? When Samuel confronted him, what reasons did he give?

In verse 20, what specific issue concerned him? How does this apply to High I's?

A Look Ahead

In the next lesson, we will look at what causes a High I to react to stress in the way that he does. In addition, we will suggest ways you can help the High I's. Finally, we will study how Jesus dealt with Peter to help him become the type of leader He needed.

RESPONDING TO THE NEEDS OF THE INFLUENCING PERSONALITY

Assignment:

Understanding How Others Misunderstand You,
chapter 8, pp. 143-63

If you are to understand how to love a High I, you must first be aware of what typically happens to a High I when certain of his needs are not met. High I's want to be surrounded by people who come together in a positive, friendly environment. High I's enjoy situations that allow verbal interaction along with stimulating and fun activities. High I's fear social rejection. When that type of pressure presents itself, the High I will frequently bend with the pressure in order to maintain relationships. Whereas the High D will be concerned with accomplishing a set of goals, the High I will focus on reaching out to people.

In this session we will look at the situations that commonly cause the High I to cave in to pressure. We will study a biblical case study that shows a High I in a typical series of stressful events that resulted in a nongrowth experience for all those involved in the situation.

We will also look at the elements that are necessary to give the High I the best opportunity to grow. In addition, we will review a biblical case study in which Jesus created a specific environment for Peter so that he had the opportunity to work through his negative traits and mature. You will have the chance to interact with a series of questions focusing on the needs of the High I. The purpose of this exercise is to build an awareness of who the High I is and how you can be more effective in loving him.

Understanding High I Stress

Need issues: • Maintaining a positive, social relationship with peers

The High I begins to encounter stress when

1. Clear instructions arc given by a superior requiring specific action of the High I
2. The High I gives hearty *agreement* and *commitment* to the superior
3. Later, the *High I's peers* present a different set of ideas that are in total disagreement with the superior's instructions
4. Rather than communicate previous commitments, the I *caves in to social pressure* and takes action on the peers' desires
5. The superior then confronts the I on the reasons for the change
6. Using his verbal skills, the I responds by *shifting blame to others*

Biblical Case Study:
Exodus 20:2-4; 24:3, 8, 12-14; 32:1-6, 21-24

Read the Scripture passages. How would you interpret the first two commandments God gave Moses? What was the response of the nation of Israel to those commandments? What was Aaron's responsibility?

Later, in Exodus 32, what did the people ask Aaron to do? What could he have done? When Moses confronted Aaron concerning his action, how did Aaron respond? What I tendencies are apparent?

Understanding the High I Environment

1. High I's respond best to a *favorable* and *friendly* environment
2. High I's need time for *stimulating* and *fun* activities
3. High I's need opportunities to *express* their own ideas
4. You need to provide the High I with ideas for transferring *talk* into *action*
5. In dealing with High I's, always consider their need for *social* recognition
6. Try to focus discussions on *people* and *ideas,* not on *details* and *tasks*
7. Be aware that High I's commonly use a *shift-blame* strategy in a negative environment.
8. Therefore, when using confrontation with a High I, *never* ask him to answer *why* questions

Assignment

If you know a High I, have him review the list above. Have him pick at least one element that is important and meaningful in creating a loving environment for him. Record his response.

Optional Exercise

To me, the most interesting element of the High I environment is:

Understanding Christ's style of loving Peter

Read John 21:1-23. In the left column, describe Christ's actions and/or Peter's reactions. In the right column, describe the environment that Jesus created as He spoke to Peter. How do Jesus' actions compare with the suggestions given on the previous page for loving the High I profiles?

Christ's actions and Peter's reactions	The environment Jesus created
John 21:1-3 (Peter's actions)	Environment in the boat
John 21:4-6 (Christ's actions)	Environment created by Jesus
John 21:7 (Peter's reaction)	
John 21:9-13 (Christ's actions)	
John 21:15a, 16a, 17a, 18, 19 (Christ's actions)	
John 21:15b, 16b, 17b (Peter's reactions)	
John 21:15c, 16c, 17c (Christ's actions)	
John 21:20-23 (Christ's actions)	

Discovering the High I:
Worksheet for High I Profiles

This worksheet and the worksheet that immediately follows go together and should be discussed by specific groups. High I profiles should use this worksheet; Low I profiles (D's, S's, and C's) should use the worksheet on the next page.

After you have answered all the questions, share your answers with your partner, discussing your responses to question 1, then question 2, and so on. If you are using a discussion group method, select a spokesman to share the consensus of the group's findings. Then join the other three profiles for the group discussion.

1a. If I had to describe my behavior in three phrases, I would choose the following words

1b. I like jobs that have tasks which involve

1c. but would rather delegate tasks that involved

2. If I could select three elements to incorporate into a loving environment for me, they would be

3. As I reflect on the environment Jesus created for Peter in John 21, He would also have ministered to me when He

4a. When I am under stress, the most loving thing you can do for me is

4b. I best deal with personal anger by

5. In order to develop better relationships with the other profiles, I continually need to work on the following areas of my behavioral style:

In relating to the High D

In relating to the High S

In relating to the High C

Loving the High I:
Worksheet for Low I Profiles

This worksheet is to be filled out by the Low I profiles (D's, S's, and C's) at the same time the High I's are filling out their worksheet. After you have answered all of the questions, share your answers. If you are using a discussion group method, divide into at least three groups (High D's, High S's, and High C's) and select a spokesman for each group. Rejoin the High I's and share the consensus of the group's findings, discussing one question at a time, alternating between the High I worksheet and the Low I worksheet.

1. The areas of my life where I need the gifts of the High I are:

2. As I reflect on the environment the High I needs, the most difficult element for me to create and communicate is:

3. The one element Jesus used in John 21 that I have never tried in loving the High I, but am willing to try, is:

4. As I focus on the differences in my style and that of the High I, I see the greatest *potential* for conflict to be:

   because

5. In order to build a better personal and working relationship with High I's, I need to be willing to modify my need to/for:

Bonus question:

6. If I were planning a date or other function for a High I, I would include the following activities:

UNDERSTANDING THE STEADINESS STYLE

Assignment:
Understanding How Others Misunderstand You,
chapter 9, pp. 165-83

The **Steadiness** or **High S** individual is characterized by a more laid-back approach to life. High S's tend to be more introverted and generally possess good listening skills. High S's generally remain calm during stressful situations and patiently go about their work in an orderly manner. Whereas High I's desire public recognition, High S's prefer to stay behind the scenes. Whereas High D's operate well in an unfavorable environment, High S's prefer a predictable, stable climate.

In this session we will focus on how the Steadiness profile tends to be misunderstood by those who are different from them. Our goal is to understand why High S's respond the way they do and to gain insights into how to support them.

In addition, you will learn the basic tendencies of the High S family of Classical Patterns: **Specialist**, **Achiever**, **Agent**, and **Investigator**. You will also discover which biblical characters represent each of the four High S groups.

Understanding High S Tendencies and Skills

Basic Tendencies

1. High S's take a *pragmatic* approach to problem solving and prefer to be *team* players.
2. High S's put a high value on the *stability* of the *home.*
3. High S's are motivated by *traditional* procedures.
4. The basic fears of the High S are *conflict* and *loss of stability.*
5. High S's prefer their lives to be characterized by *order* and *tranquility.*

Basic Skills

The High S has many unique skills, but if these skills are unchecked, imbalance can occur. To counterbalance the High S's skills, a complementary DiC skill is needed. Below are examples of various High S skills and the corresponding balancing skills in the other profiles. Notice that in the last column the final three complementary profiles have been left out. Which profiles do you think should go there?

Skills of the High S Profile	Complementary skills needed by the High S	Profiles who have the complementary skills
Tends to	*Needs others who*	
Be patient	Have high energy levels	D
Be a good listener	Express the feelings of others	I
Create harmony	Focus on quality control	C
Be cooperative	Apply pressure on others	
Specialize	Handle variety and change	
Calm others	Are good at critical thinking	

Understanding How the High S Relates to Others

The following compatibility chart identifies the natural manner in which a Steadiness person generally relates to each DiSC behavioral style in personal relationships and in work settings.

Styles	Excellent 1 2	Good 3 4	Fair 5 6	Poor 7 8
S-D	W		P	
S-i	W		P	
S-S	P	W		
S-C	P W			

KEY

P = Personal Relationships
W = Work Tasks

1 = Best Possible
8 = Poorest Possible

Definitions—

S-D Team: High D's have good start-up skills and High S's have good follow-up skills. Personal relationships tend to be fair due to the fact that High S individuals desire reassurances and prefer close relationships, whereas High D individuals tend to be more independent, resist closeness, and frequently create disharmony.

S-I Team: High I's are spontaneous and desire harmony but have difficulty maintaining their focus. They also often lack follow-through. The relationship between the High I and the High S frequently becomes strained because the High S desires stability and status quo, whereas the High I needs spontaneity and change.

S-S Team: High S's get along with other High S's because they both respond to stability and family values. They can work well if they can overcome a tendency toward putting off responsibilities.

S-C Team: The High C will generally be more concerned about the task at hand, whereas the High S will be concerned with getting along with others. Those two approaches are generally congruent skills in work situations. High S's and High C's generally relate well to each other because both are committed to maintaining harmony and the status quo.

Misunderstanding the High S

Study the characteristics below and circle the traits that, in your opinion, could tend to cause misunderstandings.

Characteristics of the High S

1. *Steadiness tendencies include:*
   sitting or staying in one place
   one task at a time
   a predictable work pattern

2. *Desires an environment with:*
   status quo unless given reasons
      for change
   traditional procedures
   time to adjust to change

3. *Management style:*
   desires feedback from others
   allows others freedom to
      operate
   establishes and follows
      procedures

Characteristics of the other DiSC styles

Tendencies of the other DiSC styles:
High D styles: want to create change often
High I styles: desire varied activities
High C styles: like things in their right place

Desires an environment with:
High D styles: challenging and varying
                activities
High I styles: unstructured activities
High C styles: no sudden or abrupt changes

Management style:
High D styles: autocratic and authoritative
High I styles: democratic and informal

High C styles: bureaucratic, going by the
                book

Exploring exercise:

1. Study the characteristics of each of the High S Classical Profiles and compare them with the other DiSC styles. In your opinion, where do you feel major conflict would most likely occur?

in the S/D combination:

in the S/I combination:

in the S/C combination:

2. In your opinion, which combinations have the greatest potential for misunderstanding? Which have the least?

Understanding High S Classical Patterns

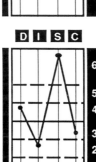

Specialist — **Isaac, Dorcas***

1-GOAL:	Status quo; controlled environment	Genesis 24:63-67
2-UNDER PRESSURE:	Becomes adaptable to those in authority	Genesis 26:1-6
3-VALUE TO THE ORGANIZATION:	Maintains the pace; behind the scenes service	Genesis 35:28-29 Acts 9:36-38
4-FEARS:	Confrontation; change; disorganization	Genesis 26:7-32 Genesis 26:34-35

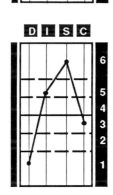

Achiever — **Nehemiah, Martha***

1-EMOTIONS:	Industrious; diligent; task oriented	Nehemiah 2:5-10 Luke 10:38-42
2-INFLUENCES OTHERS BY:	Leads by example	Nehemiah 5:14-18
3-VALUE TO THE ORGANIZATION:	Completes the task which is assigned	Nehemiah 6:15
4-INCREASE EFFECTIVENESS WITH MORE:	Reduction of ''either-or'' thinking; moderation in approach to task; ability to compromise	Nehemiah 13:23-25 John 11:20-28

Agent — **Abraham, Hannah**

1-EMOTIONS:	Accepts affection; rejects aggression	Genesis 14:17-20 Genesis 16:5-6
2-INFLUENCES OTHERS BY:	Friendship; hospitality	Genesis 18:1-8
3-VALUE TO THE ORGANIZATION:	Loyalty of service toward those who have shown him kindness	Genesis 22:1-18 1 Samuel 1:17-38; 2:11
4-UNDER PRESSURE:	Internalizes pressure; may have problems with digestion	Genesis 21:8-18 1 Samuel 1:1-11
5-FEARS:	Dissension and conflict	Genesis 12:11-13; 20:1-2 Genesis 13:7-9

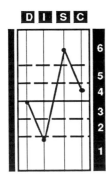

Investigator — **Jacob, James (Acts 15), Anna***

1-GOAL:	Determined	Genesis 29:15-30
2-INFLUENCES OTHERS BY:	Determination; tenacity; consistency of performance	Genesis 32:24-30 Luke 2:35-38
3-VALUE TO THE ORGANIZATION:	Working through complex problems or situations over a long period of time	Genesis 30:25-43
4-UNDER PRESSURE:	Remembers wrong done to him; tends to internalize conflict	Genesis 31:26-41 Genesis 32:1-11

*Tendencies indicate a pattern, but not enough scriptural content to make a confident association.

High S Discovery Exercise

In your opinion, how is the High S different from the High D and the High I?

How are the High S Classical Patterns different from one another?

Specialist

Achiever

Agent

Investigator

High S's are uncomfortable with *change* and fear *dissension* and *conflict*. A predictable response for High S profiles is to avoid confrontation if possible.

Read Genesis 26:1-22. Describe how Isaac handled potential conflict. How does his behavior demonstrate High S tendencies?

A Look Ahead

In the next lesson we will look at what causes High S's to react to stress in the way that they do. In addition, we will look at what you can do to help them. Finally, we will study how the Lord supported Abraham.

RESPONDING TO THE NEEDS OF THE STEADINESS PERSONALITY

Assignment:
Understanding How Others Misunderstand You,
chapter 10, pp. 185-203

To understand how to love the High S, you must first understand what happens to a High S when certain of his needs are not met. As with other profiles, High S's will protect themselves, and their reactions are predictable. Specifically, the High S needs a stable environment free of conflict. When the opposite condition is present High S profiles become uncomfortable, internalize the pressure, and begin to withdraw. Whereas the High D becomes aggressive when he is under pressure, the High S will flee and go into a shell. Whereas the High I becomes emotional and talkative under pressure, the High S becomes unemotional and quiet.

In this session, we will describe situations that commonly cause the High S profile to react in the way we outlined above. In addition, we will look at a biblical case study that amplifies what typically happens.

We will also look at the elements that are necessary to give the High S the best opportunity to grow through stressful situations. In addition, you will be asked to review a biblical case study in which God provides Abraham with the positive elements he needs to naturally grow in his trust in the Lord. Finally, you will be given the opportunity to test the concepts presented in this session through responding to a series of questions designed for small group discussion.

Understanding High S Stress

Need issues:
• An environment free of conflict (particularly within the home)
• Time to adjust to change

The High S begins to encounter stress when his

1. Routine action does not create the expected *results*
2. The S's partner then implements an aggressive "take control" strategy
3. The S typically complies, but produces only *passive results*
4. The S's partner then uses stronger *confrontive* measures, thinking that *more pressure* is an even better strategy
5. This results in the S's adopting a *passive-aggressive* response, i.e., *noninvolvement, silence,* or the *turtle syndrome*

Biblical Case Study: Genesis 15:1-5; 16:1-6

Read the Scripture passages and determine the promise God gave Abraham. Describe Sarah's response to God's plan when she speaks to Abraham in Genesis 16. Describe Abraham's reaction. (Remember, Sarah is a D, and Abraham is an S.)

Confrontation and Pressure

Understanding the High S Environment

1. High S's respond best in an environment that maintains the *status quo* unless reasons are given for *change*. If change is necessary, present ideas in a *nonthreatening* manner.
2. Give the High S a chance to *adjust* to *change*.
3. Be aware of his need for *security* within the family.
4. Allow the High S the time and opportunity to *visualize, touch,* and *experience* an orderly transition before assuming ownership of change.
5. Provide personal *assurances* of *support*.
6. Provide a *sincere, personal* and *agreeable* environment.
7. Be *patient* in drawing out his goals.

Assignment

If you know a High S, have him review the list above and pick at least one element that is important and meaningful in creating a loving environment for him. Record his response.

Optional Exercise

To me, the most interesting element of the High S environment is:

"Isn't there an easier way?!!"

Understanding God's style of loving Abraham

Study the following passages of Scripture. In the left column, describe the Lord's actions and Abraham's reaction. In the right column, describe the environment God created as He spoke to Abraham. How does it compare to the model given on the previous pages?

The Lord's actions and Abraham's reactions	The environment the Lord created
Acts 7:2-5; Joshua 24:2-3	
Genesis 11:31-32	
Genesis 12:1-7	
Genesis 13:1-4	
Genesis 15:1-6	
Genesis 17:1-22	
Genesis 22:1-12	

Discovering the High S:
Worksheet for High S Profiles

    This worksheet and the worksheet that immediately follows go together and should be discussed by specific groups. High S profiles should use this worksheet; Low S profiles (D's, I's, and C's) should use the worksheet on the next page.

    After you have answered all the questions, share your answers with your partner, discussing your responses to question 1, then question 2, and so on. If you are using a discussion group method, select a spokesman to share the consensus of the group's findings. Then join the other three profiles for the group discussion.

    1a. If I had to describe my behavior in three phrases, I would choose the following words

    1b. I like jobs which have tasks that include

    1c. but I would rather delegate tasks involving

    2. If I could select three key elements to incorporate into a loving environment for me, they would be

    3. As I reflect on the environment God created for Abraham, He would also have ministered to me personally when He

    4a. When I am under stress, the most loving thing you can do for me is

    4b. I have learned to overcome my need for the status quo by

    5. In order to develop better relationships with the other profiles, I continually need to work on the following areas of my behavioral style:

In relating to the High D

In relating to the High I

In relating to the High C

Loving the High S:
Worksheet for Low S Profiles

This worksheet is to be filled out by the Low S profiles (D's, I's, and C's) at the same time the High S's are filling out their worksheet. After you have answered all of the questions, share your answers. If you are using a discussion group method, divide into at least three groups (High D's, High I's, and High C's) and select a spokesman for each group. Rejoin the High S's and share the consensus of the group's findings, discussing one question at a time, alternating between the High S worksheet and the Low S worksheet.

1. The areas of my life where I need the gifts of the High S are:

2. As I reflect on God's style in loving Abraham, the most difficult element for me to project is:

3. The one element I have never tried in loving the High S, but will try to implement the next time I deal with a High S, is:

4. As I review the differences in my style and that of the High S, I see the greatest *potential* for conflict to be:

   because

5. In order to build a harmonious working and personal relationship with a High S, I need to be willing to modify my need to/for:

Bonus question:

6. If I were planning a date or other function for a High S, I would include the following activities:

UNDERSTANDING THE COMPLIANT STYLE

Assignment:
Understanding How Others Misunderstand You,
chapter 11, pp. 205-24

Compliant, or **High C**, individuals have concern for detail and quality control. They tend to be critical thinkers and check for accuracy. Whereas High I's tend to be extremely forgiving of personal errors, High C's have a tendency to remember their mistakes and be self-critical. Whereas the High D will behave aggressively in an unfavorable environment, the High C will respond more cautiously. Whereas the High S will initially focus on the relational issues, the High C will focus on tasks.

In this lesson we will focus on how the Compliant style relates to the other profiles. We will also study how the High C tends to be misunderstood. Our goal will be to understand why conflicts occur with the Compliant profiles and what can be done to help them work through sensitive issues in their lives. If this can be done, the High C's will be freed to mature in their walk with the Lord.

In addition, we will discuss the basic tendencies of the High C and the family of Compliant Classical Patterns: **Objective Thinker**, **Perfectionist**, and **Practitioner**. Positive biblical characters will be associated with each of the three High C groups.

Understanding High C Tendencies and Skills

Basic Tendencies

1. High C's have the tendency to be concerned with accuracy and precision.
2. Before assuming a new task, a High C will have a tendency to ask many clarification questions.
3. When assuming a new task, a High C will remain cautious. He is motivated by the "proper way" of doing things.
4. The basic fear of the High C is that someone will criticize his work.
5. When under pressure, High C's can become overcritical and demanding of themselves and others.

Basic Skills

The High C has special quality-control skills, but if these are left unchecked, imbalance can occur. To counterbalance the High C's skills a complementary DiS skill is needed. Below are various examples of High C skills along with the corresponding balancing skills in the other profiles. Notice that in the last column the final three complementary profiles have been left out. Which profiles do you think should go there?

Skills of the High C Profile	Complementary skills needed by the High C	Profiles who have the complementary skills
Tends to	*Needs others who*	
Be analytical	Make quick decisions	D
Make sure it's right	Delegate important tasks	I
Maintain quality control	Compromise on unimportant issues	S
Follow directions	Take appropriate risks	
Be reserved	Have the ability to interact with others	
Take a sensitive approach	Have a sense of humor; are laid back	

Used by permission of Carlson Learning Company.

81

Understanding How the High C
Relates to Others

The following compatibility chart identifies the natural manner in which a Compliant person generally relates to each DiSC behavioral style in personal relationships and in work settings.

Styles	Excellent 1 2	Good 3 4	Fair 5 6	Poor 7 8
C-D			W	P
C-i		W		P
C-S	P W			
C-C	P	W		

KEY

P = Personal
      Relationships
W = Work Tasks

1 = Best Possible
8 = Poorest
      Possible

Definitions—

C-D Team: The C's and D's have the most *potential* difficulty in working and relating together because of differences in expectations. The C's generally expect standards and rules to be followed whereas the D's have a "the end justifies the means" outlook. Both need each other and if they can resolve their expectation differences, they can become an effective team.

C-I Team: The work relationship between C and I is generally good because the C's generally lack the interpersonal skills of the High I. In contrast, the I's need the quality control skills of the C's to keep them out of trouble. Like the D/C combination, their personal relationship often suffers because of their differences in expectations. However, the issues are different. The C's hear the I's make verbal commitments and expect them to follow through; however, the I's intent is generally just to verbalize their thoughts.

C-S Team: The C's and S's relate and work well together because both are committed to maintain the environment and keeping the status quo. The C's offer the quality control, whereas the S's see to it that the work gets done in a timely manner.

C-C Team: The C's relate well to other C's because both share similar levels of sensitivity and concerns. Their work relationship is "good" but may have difficulties in completing projects on time because of their concern for "perfection." If production schedules are critical, it's best to team them with High S profiles.

Used by permission of Carlson Learning Company.

Misunderstanding the High C

Study the characteristics below and circle the traits that, in your opinion, could tend to cause misunderstandings.

Characteristics of the High C

1. *Compliance tendencies include:*
   complying with authority
   concentrating on key details
   working under known
   circumstances

2. *Desires an environment with:*
   security assurance
   reassurances
   no sudden or abrupt changes

3. *Response to stress:*
   internalizes anger
   desires to be alone, withdraws
   becomes worrisome, becomes
   depressed

Characteristics of the other DiSC styles

Tendencies of the other DiSC styles:
High D styles: taking authority
High I styles: desiring to help others
High S styles: demonstrating patience

Desires an environment with:
High D styles: "living on the edge"
High I styles: favorable working conditions
High S styles: traditional procedures

Response to stress:
High D styles: explosive anger
High I styles: wants to talk about it
High S styles: retreats into a shell, takes a
nap

Exploring exercise:

1. Study each of the three High "C" characteristics and compare them with the other DiSC styles. In your opinion, where do you feel major conflict would most likely occur?

in the C/D combination:

in the C/I combination:

in the C/S combination:

2. In your opinion, which combinations have the greatest potential for misunderstanding? Which have the least?

Understanding High C Classical Patterns

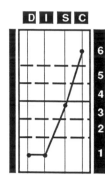

Objective Thinker

Luke, Ruth, Mary

1-GOAL:	Correctness	Luke 1:1-2
2-INFLUENCES OTHERS BY:	Factual data; logical arguments	Luke 1:3-4
3-VALUE TO THE ORGANIZATION:	Defines; clarifies; obtains information; evaluates; tests	Luke 1:26-56 (Mary's behavior)
4-OVERUSES:	Analysis	Luke 2:19

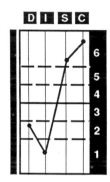

Perfectionist

Moses, John, Esther

1-EMOTIONS:	Competent; doing things right; restrained; cautious; asks clarification questions	Exodus 3:10–4:13
2-INFLUENCES OTHERS BY:	Attention to details and accuracy	Exodus 24:3-8
3-VALUE TO THE ORGANIZATION:	Deeply concerned with quality control; maintains standards	Exodus 32 Numbers 16 Deuteronomy
4-UNDER PRESSURE:	Becomes tactful and diplomatic	Exodus 4:10, 13, 18 Exodus 8:8-10

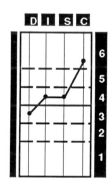

Practitioner

Elijah, Jonah, Deborah*

1-EMOTIONS:	Feels able to match or surpass in effort and technical performance	1 Kings 18:25-40
2-INFLUENCES OTHERS BY:	Developing proper procedures and verbalizing correctness	1 Kings 18:20-24
3-UNDER PRESSURE:	Becomes restrained; sensitive to criticism	1 Kings 19:1-4
4-OVERUSES:	Unrealistic expectations	1 Kings 19:5-18

*Tendencies indicate a pattern, but not enough scriptural content to make a confident association.

High C Discovery Exercise

In your opinion, how is the High C different from the High D, High I, and High S?

How are the High C Classical Patterns distinct from one another?

Objective Thinker

Perfectionist

Practitioner

High C's are sensitive to criticism and can express feelings of being all alone in the problem. Left unchecked, they can experience depression and even have thoughts of suicide.

Read 1 Kings 18:16-40; 19:21. Describe the contest Elijah proposed to Ahab and the priests of Baal. How did the contest conclude?

In 1 Kings 19, how did Jezebel feel toward Elijah? How did Elijah respond? What did he want to do? What was God's response? How does Elijah's behavior reflect High C tendencies?

A Look Ahead

In the next lesson we will look at what causes High C's to react to pressure the way they do. In addition, we will suggest ways you can help them. Finally, we will study the way God dealt with Moses, helping him become His spokesman to Pharaoh.

RESPONDING TO THE NEEDS OF THE COMPLIANT PERSONALITY

Assignment:
Understanding How Others Misunderstand You,
chapter 12, pp. 225-48

If you are to understand how to love the High C, you must first understand what happens to a High C when certain of his needs are not met. High C's desire a controlled, defined work environment that offers reassurance and security. Because God has given High C's perfectionist tendencies and expectations, they can be very hard on themselves. High C's tend to personalize negative information and are extremely sensitive to criticism.

Whereas the High D becomes aggressively intense if he is criticized, the High C becomes introspective. Whereas criticism may cause the High I to become emotional and attack, it causes the High C to become quiet and stoic. Whereas the High S retreats into a shell when he is criticized, the High C may have a total self-image breakdown. All these responses are predictable and normal for the respective profiles when they encounter criticism.

In this lesson we will study the situations that commonly cause High C profiles to respond in the manner outlined above. In addition, we will look at a biblical case study in which Israel criticized the Lord and Moses, a High C.

Most important, we will look at what elements are necessary to give the High C the best chance to handle situations that are stressful for him. In addition, we will review a biblical case study in which God created a specific environment for Moses so that he had the opportunity to begin the process of dealing with these issues. Finally, through a series of questions designed for small group discussion you will be given the opportunity to test the concepts presented in the lesson.

Understanding High C Stress

Need issues:
• Order and defined responsibility
• Reassurances of support

The High C begins to encounter stress when

1. Someone changes his plans and/or criticizes the High C's work
2. The change in plans commonly causes the High C to ask many "what about" and "what if" questions
3. Continued criticism causes feelings of hopelessness, inadequacy, and being totally alone
4. If the High C's partner becomes impatient with the continuous reservoir of questions and projects a critical spirit, the High C has a tendency to take it personally
5. The High C can also have a total self-image breakdown, a "poor me" attitude, and/or even thoughts of suicide

Biblical Case Study: Numbers 11:1-15

Read the Scripture above and describe how some of the people felt about the food God provided for them. Describe Moses' response to their complaints. What did he do? What was his solution to the problem? What C tendencies are present?

Understanding the High C Environment

1. High C's desire *personal* attention and an *exact* job description and information as to where they *fit* into the picture.
2. Allow the High C the freedom to ask clarification *questions.*
3. Be prepared to answer the *questions* in a *patient* and *persistent* manner.
4. Provide *reassurance* that no *surprises* will occur.
5. If you must disagree, disagree with the *facts,* not the person; strongly reject "*poor-me*" comments.
6. Give a High C the *time* and the opportunity to discuss changes with individuals he respects.
7. Give the High C the freedom to gain *permission* from third parties in making decisions, particularly involving changes.

Assignment

If you know a High C, have him review the list above. Have the High C pick at least one element that is important and meaningful in creating a loving environment for him. Record his response.

Optional Exercise

To me, the most interesting element of the High C environment is:

Understanding God's style of loving Moses

Study the following passages of Scripture. In the left column, describe the Lord's actions and Moses' reaction. In the right column, describe the environment God created as He spoke to Moses. How does it compare to the suggestions given on the previous page for loving High C profiles?

The Lord's actions and Moses' reactions	The environment the Lord created
Exodus 3:1-10	
Exodus 3:11 (Moses)	
Exodus 3:12	
Exodus 3:13 (Moscs)	
Exodus 3:14-22	
Exodus 4:1 (Moses)	
Exodus 4:2-9	
Exodus 4:10 (Moses)	
Exodus 4:11-12	
Exodus 4:13 (Moses)	
Exodus 4:14-18	

Discovering the High C:
Worksheet for High C Profiles

This worksheet and the worksheet that immediately follows go together and should be discussed by specific groups. High C profiles should use this worksheet; Low C profiles (D's, I's, and S's) should use the worksheet on the next page.

After you have answered all the questions, share your answers with your partner, discussing your responses to question 1, then question 2, and so on. If you are using a discussion group method, select a spokesman to share the consensus of the group's findings. Then join the other three profiles for the group discussion.

1a. If I had to describe my behavior in three phrases, I would choose the following words

1b. I like jobs that have tasks which include

1c. but would rather delegate tasks that involve

2. If I could select three key elements to incorporate into a loving environment for me, they would be

3. As I reflect on the environment God created for Moses in Exodus 3 and 4, He would also have ministered to me when He

4a. When I am under stress, the most loving thing you can do for me is

4b. I have learned to handle my high expectations of myself by

5. In order to develop better relationships with the other profiles, I continually need to work on the following areas of my behavioral style:

In relating to the High D

In relating to the High I

In relating to the High S

Loving the High C:
Worksheet for Low C Profiles

This worksheet is to be filled out by the Low C profiles (D's, I's, and S's) at the same time the High C's are filling out their worksheet. After you have answered all of the questions, share your answers, discussing your responses to question 1, then question 2, and so on. If you are using a discussion group method, divide into at least three groups (High D's, High I's, and High S's) and select a spokesman for each group. Rejoin the High C's and share the consensus of the group's findings, discussing one question at a time, alternating between the High C worksheet and the Low C worksheet.

1. Areas of my life where I need the gifts of the High C are:

2. As I reflect on the environment for the High C, the most difficult for me to create and communicate is:

3. The one element the Lord used in Exodus 3-4 that I have never used in loving the High C but am willing to try is:

4. As I review my differences in style with the High C, I see my greatest *potential* conflict to be:

5. In order to build a harmonious working and personal relationship with a High C, I need to be willing to modify my need to/for:

Bonus question:

6. If I were planning a date or other function for a High C, I would include the following activities:

MEASURING THE MATURITY OF DiSC PROFILES

Assignment:
Understanding How Others Misunderstand You,
chapter 13, pp. 249-64

Matthew 22:37

And He said to him, **You shall love the Lord your God with all your heart, and with all your soul, and with all your mind.**

One of the measurements of a person's maturity is how well he handles stress in a way that is contrary to his natural negative bent. Normally, making such an adjustment requires of the person that he make a choice between his need system (DiSC) and his value system (TISC*). The difference between a need system response and a value system response will be discussed in this session along with biblical examples.

This final session will be devoted to explaining how positive changes can take place within the DiSC models. The testimonies will be those of Peter, Paul, Abraham, and Moses, showing how they successfully handled stress issues that earlier in their lives had caused them to fail. This same potential is available to us all.

* An acronym for *Traditionalist, In-betweener, Challenger, Sythesizer.*

Needs versus Values

DiSC System	TISC System
Dominance	Traditionalist
Influencing	In-betweener
Steadiness	Challenger
Compliance	Synthesizer

Needs   versus   Values

Motivated behavior (The DiSC system)	Motivated behavior (The TISC system)
The **would do's** of life	The **should do's** of life
What is **comfortable**	What is **right**
What is **easiest**	What is most **reasonable**
What **works**	What is most **meaningful**
What is **most natural** for us	What **others expect** of us (or what we expect of ourselves)

Measuring the Maturity of the High S

Fears of the High S: • Giving up *security* and *conflict*

Defensive response: • Maintain *status quo* and avoid pain by employing a *passive-aggressive* strategy

Case study: Abraham (Genesis 22:1-3, 9-10)

In this passage, God asks Abraham to offer up his son Isaac. The normal response of a High S would be to busy himself doing other things and ignore the message. If pushed on the issue, a High S would be likely to suggest a compromise but avoid making a decision. Contrast the actions of Abraham with the natural fears of the High S. **What risk do you see Abraham taking?**

> Now it came about after these things, that God tested Abraham, and said to him, "Abraham!" And he said, "Here I am."
>
> And He said, "Take now your son, your only son, whom you love, Isaac, and go to the land of Moriah; and offer him there as a burnt offering on one of the mountains of which I will tell you."
>
> So Abraham rose early in the morning and saddled his donkey, and took two of his young men with him and Isaac his son; and he split wood for the burnt offering, and arose and went to the place of which God had told him.
>
> Then they came to the place of which God had told him; and Abraham built the altar there, and arranged the wood, and bound his son Isaac, and laid him on the altar on top of the wood.
>
> And Abraham stretched out his hand, and took the knife to slay his son.

Measuring the Maturity of the High C

Fears of the High C: • Making unpopular decisions *alone*, creating *antagonism, the unknown*

Defensive response: • Move *cautiously*, ask lots of *questions*, and use a *"poor-me"* strategy as a means of not getting involved

Case study: Moses (Exodus 32:9-10, 30-33)

In this passage, God commanded Moses to proceed independently and confront Israel with its great sin of worshiping the golden calf. By using a pro and con strategy, God guided Moses toward committing himself to the assignment. However, when Moses personally saw the Israelites in the midst of this grievous sin it was obvious someone would have to go back up to God and make an atonement for it. The normal High C response would be to pray about it for several weeks, select a committee to carry the message, and then ask someone else to be the spokesman. Contrast Moses' response to the fears of the High C. **What risks did Moses take?**

> And the Lord said to Moses, "I have seen this people, and behold, they are an obstinate people.
> "Now then let Me alone, that My anger may burn against them, and that I may destroy them; and I will make of you a great nation."
> And it came about on the next day that Moses said to the people, "You yourselves have committed a great sin; and now I am going up to the Lord, perhaps I can make atonement for your sin."
> Then Moses returned to the Lord, and said, "Alas, this people has committed a great sin, and they have made a god of gold for themselves.
> "But now, if Thou wilt, forgive their sin—and if not, please blot me out from Thy book which Thou hast written!"

Worksheet

1. What risk did each of the biblical characters have to face as it related to his natural fear?

   Paul, High D:

   Peter, High I:

   Abraham, High S:

   Moses, High C:

2. Put yourself in the place of the biblical character most like you. Describe how you would have reacted.

3. If you had to list your greatest fear, what would it be?

   High D group:

   High I group:

   High S group:

   High C group:

4. If you had to face this fear, what would you recommend we do to help you?

CLASSICAL PATTERNS AND SCRIPTURE PARALLELS

Paul   the Creative Profile

Peter   the Persuader Profile

Abraham   the Agent Profile

Moses   the Perfectionist Profile

Paul, the High D

The Creative Pattern

Components of the Classical Patterns	Specific behavior amplification	Scripture reference
Emotions	Accepts aggression, may be restrained in expression	2 Cor. 10:1-7 2 Cor. 10:10 2 Cor. 11:6
Goal	Dominance, the unusual	2 Cor. 13:1-3 Gal. 2:7 Acts 9:15
Judges others by	Personal standards	Phil. 3:17 Acts 15:38
Influences others by	Setting a pace in developing systems, competitive	Gal. 2:1-10 Acts 15:1-35 1 Cor. 9:24-27
Overuses	Bluntness, critical attitude	Acts 23:1-5 Acts 23:12
Under pressure	Assertive and pioneering	Acts 9:1-2
Would increase effectiveness with more	Warmth, recognition that sanctions exist	Acts 8:3 Acts 9:1-2 Acts 9:3-19
Fears	Not being influential	Acts 6:8-12 Acts 7:54-60 Acts 8:1
Value to the organization	Initiator in bringing about change	Rom. 3:21-31 Eph. 2:8-10 Gal. 2:16

Peter, the High I

The Persuader Pattern

Components of the Classical Patterns	Specific behavior amplification	Scripture reference
Emotions	Trusts others, is enthusiastic	Matt. 16:13-16 Matt. 16:21-34
Goal	Authority, prestige	Acts 1:15 Acts 4:8-12 Acts 5:3-9
Judges others by	Ability to verbalize, flexibility	Luke 5:1-11
Influences others by	Friendly manner	Acts 3:1-8 Acts 10:19-48
Overuses	Enthusiasm, optimism in self and others	Matt. 14:26-31 Mark 9:2-7 Matt. 26:31-35
Under pressure	Becomes soft and persuadable	Gal. 2:11-21 Luke 22:54-60
Would increase effectiveness with more	Emotional control	Luke 22:61-62
Fears	Fixed environment	John 21:3 John 21:7-11
Value to the organization	Poised and confident, seller, closer	Acts 2-3 Acts 2:37-41

Abraham, the High S

The Agent Pattern

Components of the Classical Patterns	Specific behavior amplification	Scripture reference
Emotions	Accepts affection, rejects aggression	Gen. 14:17-20 Gen. 16:5-6
Goal	Acceptance	Gen. 12:6-8
Judges others by	Loyalty	Gen. 24:2
Influences others by	Offering understanding, friendship	Gen. 24:1-9 Gen. 18:1-8
Overuses	Kindness	Gen. 13:1-13
Under pressure	Becomes persuasive with factual material when necessary	Gen. 18:20-33 Gal. 2:11-21 Luke 22:54-60
Would increase effectiveness with more	Strength in knowing who he is; learning to say no	Gen. 12:1-13 Gen. 16:1-4
Fears	Dissension, conflict	Gen. 21:8-14 Gen. 12:11-13
Value to the organization	Harmonizes, supports, empathizes	Gen. 13:7-12 Gen. 24:5-9

Moses, the High C

The Perfectionist Pattern

Components of the Classical Patterns	Specific behavior amplification	Scripture reference
Emotions	Competent in doing things right, restrained, cautious	Ex. 6:30–7:1-5
Goal	Security	Ex. 3
Judges others by	Precise standards	Ex. 18:13-26
Influences others by	Predetermined manner, attention to detail	Ex. 34:27 Ex. 35:1-21
Overuses	Standard operating procedures	Ex. 18:13-16
Under pressure	Becomes tactful, diplomatic	Ex. 4:18 Ex. 5:3
Would increase effectiveness with more	Confidence and independence	Ex. 3:11, 14 Ex. 4:1, 10, 13 Ex. 32:7-32
Fears	Antagonism	Ex. 6:29–7:2
Value to the organization	Conscientious, maintains standards, quality control	Ex. 19-40 Deut. Num. 16

CREATING LOVING ENVIRONMENTS

WHICH PROFILE WOULD MAKE THE BEST MARRIAGE PARTNER FOR ME?

> *This is My commandment, that you love one another, just as I have loved you.* —**Jesus** John 15:12
>
> *Make my joy complete by being of the same mind, maintaining the same love, united in spirit, intent on one purpose.*
> *Do nothing from selfishness or empty conceit, but with humility of mind let each of you regard one another as more important than himself;*
> *Do not merely look out for your own personal interests, but also for the interest of others.* —**Paul**
> Philippians 2:2-4

One of the most frequent questions asked about the Biblical Profile Series relates to marriage compatibility. It is important to remember that the profiles of two people are not what determine a relationship's success; success comes from a couple's commitment and attitudes. Any couple, regardless of profiles, can be incompatible just as any couple can learn how to meet one another's needs.

This exercise will help you and your partner learn how to communicate your needs, and your love, to each other. Don't be surprised if your needs are very different from your partner's. The discovery is part of the excitement that comes as you learn to maximize your relationship.

Used by permission of In His Grace, Inc.

Analysis of
PARTNER PROFILES

My Profile: My Partner's Profile:

GRAPH I   ### GRAPH I

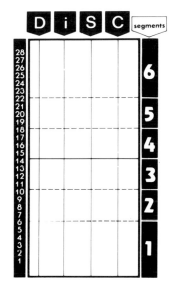   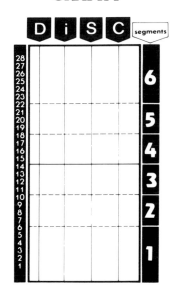

In Graph I, I am a High _____   My partner is a High _____

Profile of the Marriage:

GRAPH II

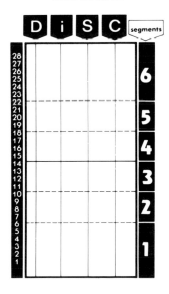

In Graph II, my partner is a High _____ Low _____
Our most similar profile is _____ Least _____

Comparisons of DiSC Profiles

Assignment: Draw a *square* around the High style that describes you and a *circle* around your partner's; compare the differences.

High D Characteristics	High I Characteristics	High S Characteristics	High C Characteristics
Tendencies include	*Tendencies include*	*Tendencies include*	*Tendencies include*
quick action, creating change, taking charge, getting results	verbalizing, generating enthusiasm	sitting or staying in one place, demonstrating patience	following directions and maintaining standards, checking for accuracy
Desires environment including	*Desires environment including*	*Desires environment including*	*Desires environment including*
freedom from controls and supervision, many varied activities	social recognition, popularity, freedom from control and detail	sincere appreciation, traditional procedures, known results	no sudden or abrupt changes, security, reassurances
Motivating needs	*Movtivating needs*	*Motivating needs*	*Motivating needs*
challenges, power and authority	flexibility, freedom of speech	stability, time to adjust to change	be part of a group, time to analyze
Fears	*Fears*	*Fears*	*Fears*
being taken advantage of	loss of social recognition	confrontation, change	irrational acts, antagonism
Judges others by	*Judges others by*	*Judges others by*	*Judges others by*
aggressiveness, results	verbal skills, flexibility	consistency, amiableness	accuracy, precise standards
Stress release	*Stress release*	*Stress release*	*Stress release*
open hostility	emotional expression of feelings	exessive need for sleep	need for time alone
Recovery needs	*Recovery needs*	*Recovery needs*	*Recovery needs*
physical time	social time	nothing time	quiet time

Communicating Differences

I feel the three best words to describe my tendencies are: (p. 7, *Biblical Personal Profile*)

If I could select three key elements to incorporate in a loving environment for me, they would be: (pp. 7, 21, *Biblical Personal Profile*)

The one area where I need help from someone else is: (p. 7, *Biblical Personal Profile*, "This person needs others who")

The one area where I need to develop is: (p. 7, *Biblical Personal Profile*, "To be more effective, this person needs")

As I review my personal Classical Pattern (Graph II), I feel the one skill I most relate to is:

Share your environment needs with your partner. Our greatest difference is

my need for _____

and my partner's need for _____

When I am under stress, the most loving thing you can do for me is to

_____

My partner's response was to _____

Profile of the Marriage

Transfer the graphs from page 105 to the specific graphs below.

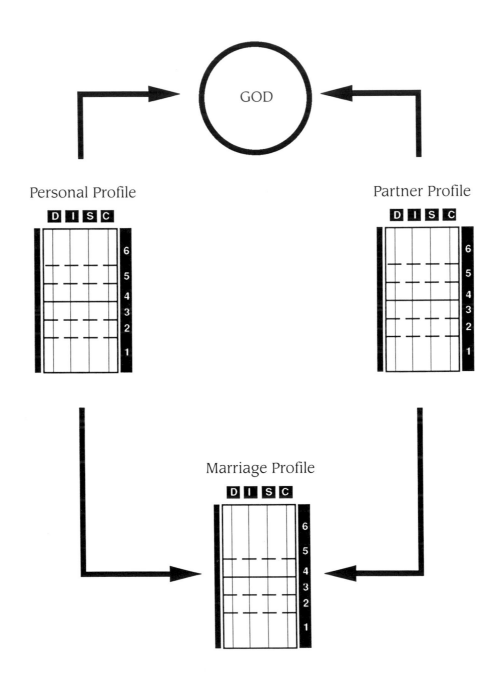

Read Genesis 2:24 and John 15. In your own words,
describe what the passages mean to you.

Used by permission of In His Grace, Inc.

THE PERSONAL PROFILE OF JESUS

What was Jesus' Personal Profile?

John 11:33-36

33 When Jesus therefore saw her weeping . . . He was deeply moved in spirit, and was troubled.
34 "Where have you laid him?" He asked.
  "Come and see, Lord," they replied.
35 Jesus wept.
36 And so the Jews were saying, "Behold how He loved him!"

One of the most frequent questions asked is "What was the personal profile of Jesus?" To answer the question, one must first arrive at a position on who He was. Jesus claimed to be God, the Son of Man. Those in His hometown reasoned He was insane. The religious leaders, Pharisees, testified before Pilate that Jesus had to be a liar. After spending three years with Him, Peter, John, and the disciples concluded that He had to be the Son of God. Scripture records that Satan and the demons agreed with the disciples. Finally, of the three recorded New Testament statements by God the Father, two directly confirm that Jesus was His Son. What is important is for you to discover who He was.

In studying the behavior of Christ, we will first look at Graph I, which deals with who Jesus was in a given circumstance. This graph typically varies depending upon the expectations of those involved. The ideal, of course, is for the individual to take on the behavior style that best meets the need of the situation. To validate Jesus' profile for yourself, study the Scripture references on page 110, which correlate to the traits found on the Intensity Index in the Biblical Profile. What do these references tell you about His ability to adapt to the need of any given situation?

DiSC Intensity Index of Jesus—Graph I

	High D Dominance **Prefers to Be in Control**	High I Influencing **Prefers Involvement with People**	High S Steadiness **Prefers Predictable Structure**	High C Compliance **Prefers Procedures and Order**	
28 27 26 25 24 23	Luke 4:8 Mark 5:1-13 Mark 1:21-27 domineering Luke 4:41 Luke 8:23-25	Matt. 14:14 Matt. 14:16-21 persuasive Matt. 14:24-33 John 4:11-30 John 3:1-21	Mark 14:26-31 patient Luke 22:31-32 Luke 22:54-61 John 21:15-19 John 20:19-31	Luke 4:3-4 accurate Luke 4:12 Matt. 4:5-12 systematic Luke 9:14-17	**6**
22 21 20 19	risk-taker Luke 11:38-54 Matt. 12:10-14 Mark 12:38-40	John 4:5-10 Luke 11:37 Luke 10:38-42 sociable	John 8:1-11 John 4:4-9 Mark 4:1-2 relaxed	Matt. 26:50-56 Mark 14:55-61 restrained John 19:7-11	**5**
18 17 16 15	self-assured Mark 11:27-33 Matt. 22:23-46 John 15:1-17	generous Mark 8:1-9 Matt. 8:1-14 Matt. 19:1-2	Luke 10:1-11 deliberate amiable Matt. 19:13-15	Luke 19:41-44 sensitive John 11:32-35 Mark 6:34	**4**
14 13 12 11	Matt. 12:14-21 Mark 7:24 unassuming Mark 5:38-43	convincing Luke 9:18-35 John 4:31-42 Luke 10:25-37	mobile Matt. 15:29-30 Matt. 19:1-2 Luke 13:22	"own-person" Luke 14:2-4 Luke 15:1-32 Matt. 16:1-4	**3**
10 9 8 7	realistic Matt. 16:13-21 Mark 9:30-31 Luke 18:31-34	factual Luke 9:43-44 Mark 10:32-34 Matt. 17:22-23	critical Matt. 15:1-9 Matt. 23:1-39 Luke 13:13-16	independent Matt. 12:1-8 Mark 7:1-8 Luke 19:45-48	**2**
6 5 4 3 2 1	John 8:10-11 mild John 12:27-28 John 6:38-40 dependent Matt. 26:37-42	Mark 1:35 Matt. 14:13 Luke 22:41 withdrawn Luke 6:12 Matt. 14:22-23	Luke 7:11-17 Luke 13:10-13 spontaneous Luke 5:1-3 Luke 5:4-11 Matt. 13:1-9	Luke 15:1-2 rebellious Mark 2:23-28 Mark 3:1-6 Luke 19:1-7 Matt. 9:9-13	**1**
	Prefers to Be a Team-Player **Low D** Dominance	**Prefers to Be Alone** **Low I** Influencing	**Prefers Variety and Change** **Low S** Steadiness	**Prefers Spontaneous Approach** **Low C** Compliance	

Christ's profiles in Graphs II and III

BPP GRAPH II

Instinctive response under pressure:

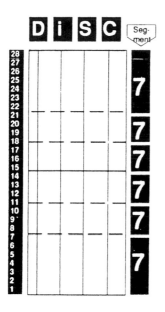

Graph II is most indicative of who a person really is. If Jesus was God, He had to be perfect.

Since the number seven represents perfection, the segment numbers were changed to indicate His Deity. However, you decide how well Jesus responded to pressure by studying the scripture references below.

High D	—John 8:12-59
Low D	—Matthew 26:36-56; John 17
High I	—John 4:1-42
Low I	—Matthew 4:1-11
High S	—John 8:1-9; Luke 22:31-34
Low S	—John 2:12-17; Matthew 21:12-17
High C	—Matthew 22:23-46
Low C	—Matthew 12:1-14

BPP GRAPH III

Self-perception

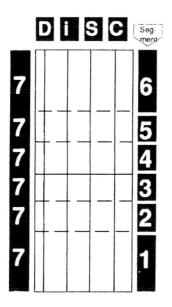

The third graph describes a person's self-perception. When asked, Jesus preferred the title "Son of Man," indicating a combination of God and Man. To indicate this on Graph III, the segment numbers on the left retain the number seven, confirming His Deity, and the segment numbers on the right (1-6), His Humanity; i.e., 100 percent God and 100 percent Man. To further your understanding of Jesus, study the conclusions of those people who knew Him the best. Who do you think Jesus was?

Paul	—Phillipians 2:5-11
Peter	—Matthew 16:13-16
Demons	—Matthew 8:29; Mark 1:24
God the Father	—Mark 1:11; Matthew 17:5
John	—John 20:30-31

Who Was Jesus?

Jesus Claimed to Be God
(John 8:58)

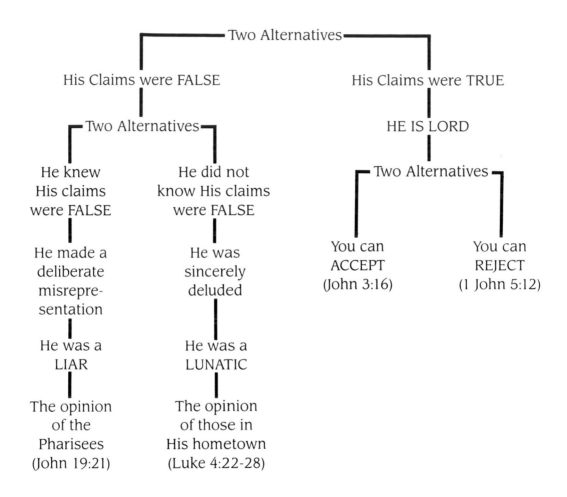

Based on your personal study, who do you believe Jesus was?

Based on John 3:16, what are the benefits of believing He was the Son of God?

APPENDIX D
RESOURCES

GENERAL

Ken Voges and Ron Braund. *Understanding How Others Misunderstand You.*
Chicago: Moody, 1990.

Ken Voges, *Biblical Personal Profiles.* Minneapolis, Minn.: Performax Systems
International, 1985. Prepared in association with In His Grace (Houston,
Texas). A product of the Carlson Learning Company.

____. *The Biblical Behavioral Series, Part A: Understanding Yourself and Others; Part
B: Creating Loving Environments.* Minneapolis, Minn.: Performax Systems
International, 1986; rev. ed., 1987. Catalog numbers C-066 and C-067.

TEACHER SUPPORT MATERIALS

John G. Grier and Dorothy E. Downey. *Adult Library of Classical Profile Patterns.* 15
vols. Minneapolis, Minn.: Carlson Learning Company; 1979.For information,
contact the Institute for Leadership Development(address below). catalog
number A-001.

____. *Child's Library of Classical Profile Patterns.* 15 vols. Minneapolis, Minn.:
Carlson Learning Company, 1983. For information, contact the Institute for
Leadership Development(address below). catalog number A-003.

Classical Styles Audio Library. 16 vols. Minneapolis, Minn.: Carlson Learning
Company, 1989. For information, contact the Institute for Leadership
Development(address below). catalog number D-026.

Complete set, *Adult and Child's Classical Profile Patterns*, including *Classical Styles
Audio Library.* A product of the Carlson Learning Company. For information,
contact the Institute for Leadership Development(address below). catalog
number A-004.

ASSESSMENT INSTRUMENTS

Information on the assessment instruments, training seminars, and the Carlson Learning Company materials may be obtained form either.

Institute for Leadership Development
2550 Windy Hill Road, Suite 321
Marietta, Georgia 30067
1-800-950-1445

In His Grace, Inc.
4822 Droddy
Houston, Texas 77091
1-713-688-1201

The assessment instruments, with their catalog numbers, are listed below:

Biblical Personal Profiles,   C-047

Personal Profile System,   C-001

Couple's Profile,   C-170

Couple's Support Guide,   C-170

Child's Discovery Profile,   C-207-F

Job Factor Analysis,   C-009

A VALUABLE INSIGHT INTO SCRIPTURAL CHARACTERS

By Ken Voges

Carlson Learning Company

IN ASSOCIATION WITH IN HIS GRACE, INC.

NAME _____ DATE _____

*Additional sheets of response forms and instructions for a second respondent
are included in this *Biblical Personal Profile.*

Choose *one* MOST and *one* LEAST in each of the 24 groups of words.

	MOST	LEAST
1		
gentle	◯	◯
persuasive	◯	◯
humble	◯	◯
original	◯	◯
2		
attractive	◯	◯
introspective	◯	◯
stubborn	◯	◯
sweet	◯	◯
3		
easily led	◯	◯
bold	◯	◯
loyal	◯	◯
charming	◯	◯
4		
open-minded	◯	◯
obliging	◯	◯
will power	◯	◯
cheerful	◯	◯
5		
jovial	◯	◯
precise	◯	◯
nervy	◯	◯
even-tempered	◯	◯
6		
competitive	◯	◯
considerate	◯	◯
joyful	◯	◯
harmonious	◯	◯

	MOST	LEAST
7		
fussy	◯	◯
obedient	◯	◯
unconquerable	◯	◯
playful	◯	◯
8		
brave	◯	◯
inspiring	◯	◯
submissive	◯	◯
timid	◯	◯
9		
sociable	◯	◯
patient	◯	◯
self-reliant	◯	◯
soft-spoken	◯	◯
10		
adventurous	◯	◯
receptive	◯	◯
cordial	◯	◯
moderate	◯	◯
11		
talkative	◯	◯
controlled	◯	◯
conventional	◯	◯
decisive	◯	◯
12		
polished	◯	◯
daring	◯	◯
diplomatic	◯	◯
satisfied	◯	◯

	MOST	LEAST
13		
aggressive	◯	◯
extroverted	◯	◯
amiable	◯	◯
fearful	◯	◯
14		
cautious	◯	◯
determined	◯	◯
convincing	◯	◯
good-natured	◯	◯
15		
willing	◯	◯
eager	◯	◯
agreeable	◯	◯
high-spirited	◯	◯
16		
confident	◯	◯
sympathetic	◯	◯
tolerant	◯	◯
assertive	◯	◯
17		
well-disciplined	◯	◯
generous	◯	◯
animated	◯	◯
persistent	◯	◯
18		
admirable	◯	◯
kind	◯	◯
resigned	◯	◯
force of character	◯	◯

	MOST	LEAST
19		
respectful	◯	◯
pioneering	◯	◯
optimistic	◯	◯
accommodating	◯	◯
20		
argumentative	◯	◯
adaptable	◯	◯
nonchalant	◯	◯
light-hearted	◯	◯
21		
trusting	◯	◯
contented	◯	◯
positive	◯	◯
peaceful	◯	◯
22		
good mixer	◯	◯
cultured	◯	◯
vigorous	◯	◯
lenient	◯	◯
23		
companionable	◯	◯
accurate	◯	◯
outspoken	◯	◯
restrained	◯	◯
24		
restless	◯	◯
neighborly	◯	◯
popular	◯	◯
devout	◯	◯

*Descriptive root words adapted from *Emotions of Normal People* by William Moulton Marsten

PAGE 2

1. responding

1. Study the first group of words on page 2 while thinking about the behavioral tendencies you show in a specific setting or focus.
   (MY SPECIFIC FOCUS IS:_____)

2. Select only one word that **MOST** describes you. Use a coin to rub over the oval after that word in the **MOST** column. A symbol will appear. See EXAMPLE 1.

3. Select *only* one word that **LEAST** describes you. Use a coin to rub over the oval after the word in the **LEAST** column. A symbol will appear.

4. Use the Same procedure to respond to the remaining groups of descriptive words.
   Remember: *Only* one **MOST** and one **LEAST** choice for each group.

EXAMPLE 1

This individual tends to be most original and least gentle in the selected setting.

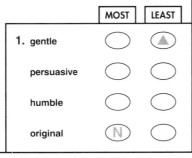

	MOST	LEAST
1. gentle	◯	◮
persuasive	◯	◯
humble	◯	◯
original	Ⓝ	◯

2. counting and recording

1. Tear out the perforated area in the lower right of this page to reveal the tally box.

2. *Most Choices:*
   Total the number of Z's in the four **MOST** columns on page 2. Write this total over the Z symbol in the **MOST** column of the tally box.

   Use the same procedure to count and record the other symbols ■ ▲ ★ N in the **MOST** columns.

3. *Least Choices:*
   Total the number of Z's in the four **LEAST** columns on page 2. Write this total over the Z symbol in the **LEAST** column of the tally box.

   Use the same procedure to count and record the other symbols ■ ▲ ★ N in the **LEAST** columns.

4. Check the accuracy by adding the **MOST** and **LEAST** columns of the tally box. Each column should total 24.

3. determining the difference

1. Determine the difference between the **MOST** and **LEAST** columns for each row of the tally box. Enter these numbers in the **DIFFERENCE** column. See EXAMPLE 2.

2. Use a plus (➕) sign if the number in the **MOST** column is greater than the number in the **LEAST** column. See example.

   Use a minus (➖) sign if the number in the **MOST** column is less than the number in the **LEAST** column.

EXAMPLE 2

TALLY BOX		
GRAPH I MOST	**GRAPH II** LEAST	**GRAPH III** DIFFERENCE
D 2	D 9	D = −7
i 0	i 8	i = −8
S 6	S 3	S = +3
C 11	C 1	C = +10
5	3	DO NOT COMPUTE
SHOULD TOTAL **24**	SHOULD TOTAL **24**	

LIFT AND TEAR PERFORATION "A" TO REVEAL

TALLY BOX

instructions
plotting

4. 1. Use the numbers from the **MOST** column of the tally box to plot Graph I. See example 3.
       Plot the **Z** number on the **D** line. ─────
       Plot the **■** number on the **i** line. ─────
       Plot the **▲** number on the **S** line. ─────
       Plot the **★** number on the **C** line. ─────
       Estimate the plotting point if a specific number is not shown on the graph. The "N" number was used to ensure accurate results and is not plotted.

    2. Use the numbers from the **LEAST** column of the tally box to plot Graph II.

    3. Use the numbers from the **DIFFERENCE** column of the tally box to plot Graph III. Note the + and — signs on **Graph III**.

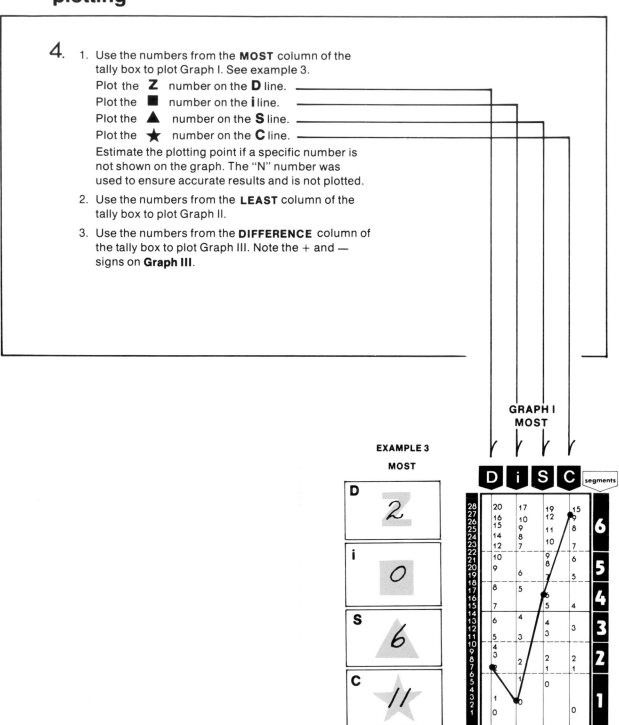

EXAMPLE 3

MOST

GRAPH I
MOST

GRAPH I behavior:
expected by others

MOST

D i S C segments

	D	i	S	C	segments
28 27 26 25 24 23	20 16 15 14 12	17 10 9 8 7	19 12 11 10	15 9 8 7	6
22 21 20 19	10 9	6	9 8 7	6 5	5
18 17 16 15	8 7	5	6 5	4	4
14 13 12 11	6 5	4 3	4 3	3	3
10 9 8 7 6	4 3 2	2	2 1	2 1	2
5 4 3 2 1	1 0	1 0	0	0	1

Segment No. _____

Pattern _____

Biblical Model _____

GRAPH II behavior:
instinctive response to pressure

LEAST

D i S C segments

	D	i	S	C	segments
28 27 26 25 24 23	0 1	0 1	0 1 2 3	0 1 2 3	6
22 21 20 19	2	2	4	4	5
18 17 16 15	3 4	3	5	5 6	4
14 13 12 11	5 6 7 8	4 5	6 7	7 8	3
10 9 8 7 6	9 10 11 12	6 7	8 9 10	9 10	2
5 4 3 2 1	13 14 15 16 21	8 9 10 11 19	11 12 13 19	11 12 13 16	1

Segment No. _____

Pattern _____

Biblical Model _____

GRAPH III behavior:
self-perception

DIFFERENCE

D i S C segments

	D	i	S	C	segments
28 27 26 25 24 23	+20 +16 +15 +14 +13 +12	+17 +9 +8 +7 +6	+19 +11 +10 +9 +8 +7	+15 +7 +6 +5 +4	6
22 21 20 19	+10 +9 +8	+5 +4 +3	+5 +4 +3	+3 +2 +1	5
18 17 16 15	+7 +5 +3 +1	+2 +1 +0	+2 +1 +0 -1	+0 -1 -2	4
14 13 12 11	+0 -2 -3	-1 -2 -3	-2 -3 -4	-3 -4 -5	3
10 9 8 7 6	-4 -6 -7 -8	-4 -5 -6	-5 -6 -7	-6 -7 -8	2
5 4 3 2 1	-9 -10 -11 -13 -14 -21	-8 -9 -10 -19	-8 -9 -10 -11 -12 -19	-9 -10 -11 -12 -16	1

Segment No. _____

Pattern _____

Biblical Model _____

1. Circle the peak of the four plotting points in Graph I. See **Example 4**

2. Use Graph II if you have two equal high points in Graph I.

3. Identify the scale for that plotting point. The example shows a high point on the **S** scale.

4. Turn to page 6.

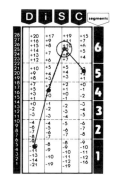

Example 4

Completed by _____

Specific Focus _____

Date _____

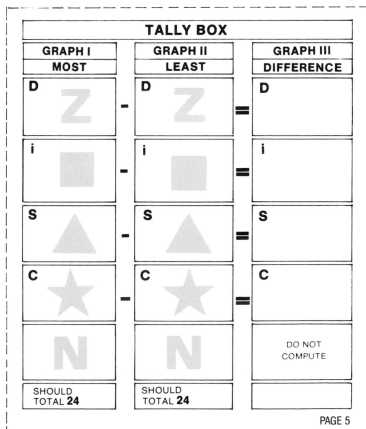

TALLY BOX

GRAPH I MOST	GRAPH II LEAST	GRAPH III DIFFERENCE
D	− D =	D
i	− i =	i
S	− S =	S
C	− C =	C
N	N	DO NOT COMPUTE
SHOULD TOTAL 24	SHOULD TOTAL 24	

PAGE 5

© Copyright 1984, Carlson Learning Company. Reprinted 1992 with permission of Carlson Learning Company. Reproduction in any form, in whole or in part, prohibited.

Biblical Personal Profiles™   119

guidelines for interpretation

The purpose of the *Biblical Profile System* is to help you *understand self and others*. Responding to the system enables you to master a framework for looking at human behavior while increasing your knowledge of your unique behavioral pattern. The goal of this practical approach is to help you create the environment which will ensure greater success for yourself. At the same time, you gain an appreciation for the different motivational environments required by those with different work behavioral styles. The interpretation, progressing from general to specific, facilitates the mastery of this individualized approach to self and others. The following summary identifies the basis for the interpretation, the interpretive content, and suggestions for use in each of the three interpretation stages.

INTERPRETATION STAGE I: GENERAL HIGHLIGHTS (page 7)

BASIS OF INTERPRETATION	INTERPRETIVE CONTENT	SUGGESTIONS FOR USE
Highest plotting point on **Graph I**	The content provides an understanding of the **D, i, S,** and **C** dimensions of behavior. The interpretation contains general highlights and includes the following. **Description:** 1. This person's tendencies include: 2. This person desires an environment which includes: **Action Plan** 1. This person needs others who: 2. To be more effective, this person needs:	Read the section indicated by your highest plotting point. **Personalize the general interpretation by:** • Underlining the phrases that describe you accurately • Deleting the phrases which do not apply • Substituting appropriate phrases from the other descriptions Read the other sections to appreciate the general differences.

INTERPRETATION STAGE II: DIMENSIONAL INTENSITY INDEX (page 8)

BASIS OF INTERPRETATION	INTERPRETIVE CONTENT	SUGGESTIONS FOR USE
The exact placement of your plotting points on the **D, i, S,** and **C** scales.	The index considers each dimension separately. The words which are revealed reflect the intensity of your tendencies on each dimension. The result is an emerging pattern of your work behavioral style.	Continue the personalization of this **more specific** interpretation. For each of the words appearing in the four columns: • Use an **x** to indicate agreement • Use an **0** to indicate disagreement • Use a **?** to indicate doubt

INTERPRETATION STAGE III: CLASSICAL PROFILE PATTERNS (pages 13 through 20)

BASIS OF INTERPRETATION	INTERPRETIVE CONTENT	SUGGESTIONS FOR USE
The interaction among the four plotting points on the **D, i, S,** and **C** scales is considered. Patterns, identified by the degree of difference in the positional relationship among the plotting points, are listed in the graph reference tables.	Consideration of the plotting point relationships for your profile graphs results in an interpretation(s) under the following headings: **emotions:** your usual "feeling" state **goal:** where you feel "right" with the world **judges others by:** the basis of your associations and hiring practices **influences others by:** your impact on others **value to the organization:** your unique contribution **overuses:** how your strengths can become weaknesses **under pressure:** often in your "blind" area **fears:** where you feel the need for protection **would increase effectiveness with more:** for maximum success	Discuss the interpretation with someone who knows you well. Continue to personalize your interpretation by matching your Classical Pattern with a Scripture character listed on Page 20. Discuss the paragraph describing your Classical Pattern with someone who has a similar profile to yours. Together study the Biblical passages which parallel your Scripture character. Read the other interpretations to increase your appreciation of people with different work behavioral styles and discover how the Lord used each profile to accomplish His work.

the library of classical profile patterns

BASIS OF INTERPRETATION	If you wish to continue the process of understanding self and others, an in-depth analysis is available. Each volume of the Library of Classical Profile Patterns focuses on one of the profile patterns. The succinct summaries contained in the Personal Profile System are expanded. Excerpts from interviews are included to illustrate how various people demonstrate these tendencies in their work settings.
GRAPH II	Comparisons between the patterns are drawn and strategies are included for working with those who are different from self. Use the pattern in Graph II if all the graphs are different.

interpretation
stage I:
general highlights

1. Read the section on **D, i, S** or **C** which correspond(s) to the scale of your highest plotting point(s) on Graph I and Graph II. Refer to Page 13 for more information about the meaning of each Graph to help you decide which is more significant for you at this time.

2. Personalize this *general* interpretation by:
   - Underlining the phrases which describe you accurately
   - Deleting the phrases which do not apply to you
   - Substituting appropriate phrases from the other descriptions

3. Read the other sections to appreciate the general differences in **D, i, S** and **C** behavioral tendencies.

 **dominance**

EMPHASIS IS ON SHAPING THE ENVIRONMENT BY OVERCOMING OPPOSITION TO ACCOMPLISH RESULTS

DESCRIPTION

This person's tendencies include:
- getting immediate results
- causing action
- accepting challenges
- making quick decisions
- questioning the status quo
- taking authority
- managing trouble
- solving problems

This person desires an environment which includes:
- power and authority
- prestige and challenge
- opportunity for individual accomplishments
- wide scope of operations
- direct answers
- opportunity for advancement
- freedom from controls and supervision
- many new and varied activities

ACTION PLAN

This person needs others who:
- weigh pros and cons
- calculate risks
- use caution
- structure a more predictable environment
- research facts
- deliberate before deciding
- recognize the needs of others

To be more effective, this person needs:
- difficult assignments
- understanding that they need people
- techniques based on practical experience
- an occasional shock
- identification with a group
- to verbalize the reasons for conclusions
- an awareness of existing sanctions
- to pace self and to relax more

---

i **influencing of others**

EMPHASIS IS ON SHAPING THE ENVIRONMENT BY BRINGING OTHERS INTO ALLIANCE TO ACCOMPLISH RESULTS

DESCRIPTION

This person's tendencies include:
- contacting people
- making a favorable impression
- verbalizing with articulateness
- creating a motivational environment
- generating enthusiasm
- entertaining people
- desiring to help others
- participating in a group

This person desires an environment which includes:
- popularity, social recognition
- public recognition of ability
- freedom of expression
- group activities outside of the job
- democratic relationships
- freedom from control and detail
- opportunity to verbalize proposals
- coaching and counseling skills
- favorable working conditions

ACTION PLAN

This person needs others who:
- concentrate on the task
- seek facts
- speak directly
- respect sincerity
- develop systematic approaches
- prefer dealing with things to dealing with people
- take a logical approach
- demonstrate individual follow-through

To be more effective, this person needs:
- control of time, if **D** or **S** is below the midline
- objectivity in decision-making
- participatory management
- more realistic appraisals of others
- priorities and deadlines
- to be more firm with others if **D** is below the midline

---

 cautiousness/compliance (to their standards)

EMPHASIS IS ON WORKING WITH EXISTING CIRCUMSTANCES TO PROMOTE QUALITY IN PRODUCTS OR SERVICE

DESCRIPTION

This person's tendencies include:
- attention to key directives and standards
- concentrating on key details
- working under known controlled circumstances
- being diplomatic with people
- checking for accuracy
- critical thinking
- critical of performance
- complying with authority

This person desires an environment which includes:
- security assurances
- standard operating procedures
- sheltered environment
- reassurance
- no sudden or abrupt changes
- being part of a work group
- personal responsiveness to their effort
- status quo unless assured of quality control
- door openers who call attention to accomplishments

ACTION PLAN

This person needs others who:
- desire to expand authority
- delegate important tasks
- make quick decisions
- use policies only as guidelines
- compromise with the opposition
- state unpopular positions

To be more effective, this person needs:
- precision work
- opportunity for careful planning
- exact job and objective descriptions
- scheduled performance appraisals
- as much respect for people's personal worth as for what they accomplish
- to develop tolerance for conflict

S **steadiness**

EMPHASIS IS ON COOPERATING WITH OTHERS TO CARRY OUT THE TASK

DESCRIPTION

This person's tendencies include:
- performing an accepted work pattern
- sitting or staying in one place
- demonstrating patience
- developing specialized skills
- concentrating on the task
- showing loyalty
- being a good listener
- calming excited people

This person desires an environment which includes:
- security of the situation
- status quo unless given reasons for change
- minimal work infringement on home life
- credit for work accomplished
- limited territory
- sincere appreciation
- identification with a group
- traditional procedures

ACTION PLAN

This person needs others who:
- react quickly to unexpected change
- stretch toward the challenges of an accepted task
- become involved in more than one thing
- are self-promoting
- apply pressure on others
- work comfortably in an unpredictable environment
- delegate to others
- are flexible in work procedures
- can contribute to the work

To be more effective, this person needs:
- conditioning prior to change
- validation of self-worth
- information on how one's efforts contribute to the total effort
- work associates of similar competence and sincerity
- guidelines for accomplishing the task
- encouragement of creativity
- confidence in the ability of others

---

interpretation stage II:
dimensional intensity index

The second stage of interpretation considers each dimension separately. The index reflects the intensity of your tendencies on the **D**, **i**, **S**, and **C** scales. To reveal your emerging behavioral pattern, use the following procedure:

1. Draw a horizontal line from the **D** plotting point to a number in the shaded bar at the left of Graph II on page 5. See **Example 5**.

2. Use the indentified number from the shaded bar to locate the corresponding number in the shaded bar of the **D** column *on this page.*

3. Use a coin to rub the space following the number. (A word will appear.)

4. Rub the three spaces below and the three spaces above this reference point. For example, if the number in the shaded bar is 5, color in 2, 3, 4, 5, 6, 7, and 8 for a total of seven spaces.

5. Follow the above procedure for the **i**, **S**, and **C** plotting points.

6. Develop **Graphs II** and **III**, if the configurations are different from **Graph I**, to reveal changes in your pattern under those conditions.

7. Personalize your interpretation:
   • Use an **x** to indicate agreement
   • Use an **O** to indicate disgreement
   • Use a **?** to indicate doubt

Example 5

D		i		S		C	
28		28		28		28	
27		27		27		27	
26		26		26		26	
25		25		25		25	
24		24		24		24	
23		23		23		23	
22		22		22		22	
21		21		21		21	
20		20		20		20	
19		19		19		19	
18		18		18		18	
17		17		17		17	
16		16		16		16	
15		15		15		15	
14		14		14		14	
13		13		13		13	
12		12		12		12	
11		11		11		11	
10		10		10		10	
9		9		9		9	
8		8		8		8	
7		7		7		7	
6		6		6		6	
5		5		5		5	
4		4		4		4	
3		3		3		3	
2		2		2		2	
1		1		1		1	

selecting the appropriate interpretation

Procedure:

 1

The Profile Graphs are divided into six segments. See arrows in Example A.

 2

The **D** plotting point is in segment 3.
The **i** plotting point is in segment 2.
The **S** plotting point is in segment 5.
The **C** plotting point is in segment 6.

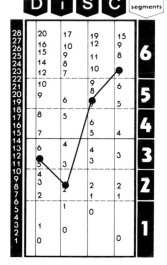

Example A

SEGMENTS **3 2 5 6**
PATTERN **Perfectionist**
Biblical Model - **Moses**

 3

The number is placed below the graph.

 4

Segment number 3256 is listed in the graph reference tables (pgs. 9 thru 12) as the Perfectionist. The title is placed below the graph. The Biblical parallel, Moses, is found on page 20.

 5

Turn to page 5 and follow the above procedure for each of the three graphs.

6

Turn to page 13 for an explanation of the graphs before reading the interpretation for each graph.

66

6666 - Overshift
6665 - Overshift
6664 - Inspirational*
6663 - Inspirational*
6662 - Inspirational*
6661 - Inspirational*
6656 - Overshift
6655 - Overshift
6654 - Inspirational*
6653 - Inspirational*
6652 - Inspirational*
6651 - Inspirational*
6646 - Inspirational*
6645 - Inspirational*
6644 - Inspirational*
6643 - Inspirational*
6642 - Inspirational*
6641 - Inspirational*
6636 - Inspirational*
6635 - Inspirational*
6634 - Inspirational*
6633 - Inspirational
6632 - Inspirational
6631 - Inspirational
6626 - Inspirational*
6625 - Inspirational*
6624 - Inspirational*
6623 - Inspirational
6622 - Inspirational
6621 - Inspirational
6616 - Inspirational*
6615 - Inspirational*
6614 - Inspirational*
6613 - Inspirational
6612 - Inspirational
6611 - Inspirational

65

6566 - Overshift
6565 - Overshift
6564 - Achiever*
6563 - Achiever*
6562 - Achiever*
6561 - Achiever*
6556 - Overshift
6555 - Overshift
6554 - Result Oriented*
6553 - Result Oriented*
6552 - Result Oriented*
6551 - Result Oriented*
6546 - Creative*
6545 - Creative*
6544 - Result Oriented*
6543 - Result Oriented*
6542 - Result Oriented*
6541 - Result Oriented*
6536 - Creative*
6535 - Creative*
6534 - Result Oriented*
6533 - Result Oriented
6532 - Result Oriented
6531 - Result Oriented
6526 - Creative*
6525 - Creative*
6524 - Result Oriented*
6523 - Result Oriented
6522 - Result Oriented
6521 - Result Oriented
6516 - Creative*
6515 - Creative*
6514 - Result Oriented*
6513 - Result Oriented
6512 - Result Oriented
6511 - Result Oriented

64

6466 - Creative*
6465 - Achiever*
6464 - Achiever*
6463 - Achiever*
6462 - Achiever*
6461 - Achiever*

6456 - Creative*
6455 - Creative*
6454 - Achiever*
6453 - Achiever*
6452 - Achiever*
6451 - Achiever*
6446 - Creative*
6445 - Creative*
6444 - Result Oriented*
6443 - Result Oriented*
6442 - Result Oriented*
6441 - Result Oriented*
6436 - Creative*
6435 - Creative*
6434 - Result Oriented*
6433 - Result Oriented
6432 - Result Oriented
6431 - Result Oriented
6426 - Creative*
6425 - Creative*
6424 - Result Oriented*
6423 - Result Oriented
6422 - Result Oriented
6421 - Result Oriented
6416 - Creative*
6415 - Creative*
6414 - Result Oriented*
6413 - Result Oriented
6412 - Result Oriented
6411 - Result Oriented

63

6366 - Creative*
6365 - Achiever*
6364 - Achiever*
6363 - Achiever*
6362 - Achiever*
6361 - Achiever*
6356 - Creative*
6355 - Creative*
6354 - Achiever*
6353 - Achiever*
6352 - Achiever*
6351 - Achiever*
6346 - Creative*
6345 - Creative*
6344 - Creative*
6343 - Achiever*
6342 - Achiever*
6341 - Achiever*
6336 - Creative
6335 - Creative
6334 - Creative
6333 - Developer
6332 - Developer
6331 - Developer
6326 - Creative
6325 - Creative
6324 - Creative
6323 - Developer
6322 - Developer
6321 - Developer
6316 - Creative
6315 - Creative
6314 - Creative
6313 - Developer
6312 - Developer
6311 - Developer

62

6266 - Creative*
6265 - Achiever*
6264 - Achiever*
6263 - Achiever*
6262 - Achiever*
6261 - Achiever*
6256 - Creative*
6255 - Creative*
6254 - Achiever*
6253 - Achiever*
6252 - Achiever*
6251 - Achiever*
6246 - Creative*
6245 - Creative*
6244 - Creative*
6243 - Achiever*
6242 - Achiever*
6241 - Achiever*
6236 - Creative

6235 - Creative
6234 - Creative
6233 - Developer
6232 - Developer
6231 - Developer
6226 - Creative
6225 - Creative
6224 - Creative
6223 - Developer
6222 - Developer
6221 - Developer
6216 - Creative
6215 - Creative
6214 - Creative
6213 - Developer
6212 - Developer
6211 - Developer

61

6166 - Creative*
6165 - Achiever*
6164 - Achiever*
6163 - Achiever*
6162 - Achiever*
6161 - Achiever*
6156 - Creative*
6155 - Creative*
6154 - Achiever*
6153 - Achiever*
6152 - Achiever*
6151 - Achiever*
6146 - Creative*
6145 - Creative*
6144 - Creative*
6143 - Achiever*
6142 - Achiever*
6141 - Achiever*
6136 - Creative
6135 - Creative
6134 - Creative
6133 - Developer
6132 - Developer
6131 - Developer
6126 - Creative
6125 - Creative
6124 - Creative
6123 - Developer
6122 - Developer
6121 - Developer
6116 - Creative
6115 - Creative
6114 - Creative
6113 - Developer
6112 - Developer
6111 - Developer

56

5666 - Overshift
5665 - Overshift
5664 - Persuader*
5663 - Persuader*
5662 - Persuader*
5661 - Persuader*
5656 - Overshift
5655 - Overshift
5654 - Persuader*
5653 - Persuader*
5652 - Persuader*
5651 - Persuader*
5646 - Appraiser*
5645 - Appraiser*
5644 - Persuader*
5643 - Persuader*
5642 - Persuader*
5641 - Persuader*
5636 - Appraiser*
5635 - Appraiser*
5634 - Persuader*
5633 - Persuader
5632 - Persuader
5631 - Persuader
5626 - Appraiser*
5625 - Appraiser*
5624 - Persuader*
5623 - Persuader
5622 - Persuader

5621 - Persuader
5616 - Appraiser*
5615 - Appraiser*
5614 - Persuader
5613 - Persuader
5612 - Persuader
5611 - Persuader

55

5566 - Overshift
5565 - Overshift
5564 - Inspirational*
5563 - Inspirational*
5562 - Inspirational*
5561 - Inspirational*
5556 - Overshift
5555 - Overshift
5554 - Inspirational*
5553 - Inspirational*
5552 - Inspirational*
5551 - Inspirational*
5546 - Appraiser*
5545 - Appraiser*
5544 - Inspirational*
5543 - Inspirational*
5542 - Inspirational*
5541 - Inspirational*
5536 - Appraiser*
5535 - Appraiser*
5534 - Inspirational*
5533 - Inspirational
5532 - Inspirational
5531 - Inspirational
5526 - Appraiser*
5525 - Appraiser*
5524 - Inspirational*
5523 - Inspirational
5522 - Inspirational
5521 - Inspirational
5516 - Appraiser*
5515 - Appraiser*
5514 - Inspirational*
5513 - Inspirational
5512 - Inspirational
5511 - Inspirational

54

5466 - Perfectionist*
5465 - Investigator*
5464 - Investigator*
5463 - Achiever*
5462 - Achiever*
5461 - Achiever*
5456 - Perfectionist*
5455 - Investigator*
5454 - Achiever*
5453 - Achiever*
5452 - Achiever*
5451 - Achiever*
5446 - Creative*
5445 - Creative*
5444 - Result Oriented*
5443 - Result Oriented*
5442 - Result Oriented*
5441 - Result Oriented*
5436 - Creative*
5435 - Creative*
5434 - Result Oriented*
5433 - Result Oriented
5432 - Result Oriented
5431 - Result Oriented
5426 - Creative*
5425 - Creative*
5424 - Result Oriented*
5423 - Result Oriented
5422 - Result Oriented
5421 - Result Oriented
5416 - Creative*
5415 - Creative*
5414 - Result Oriented*
5413 - Result Oriented
5412 - Result Oriented
5411 - Result Oriented

53

5366 - Perfectionist*
5365 - Investigator*
5364 - Investigator*
5363 - Achiever
5362 - Achiever
5361 - Achiever
5356 - Perfectionist*
5355 - Investigator*
5354 - Achiever*
5353 - Achiever
5352 - Achiever
5351 - Achiever
5346 - Creative*
5345 - Creative*
5344 - Creative*
5343 - Achiever*
5342 - Achiever*
5341 - Achiever*
5336 - Creative
5335 - Creative
5334 - Creative
5333 - Developer
5332 - Developer
5331 - Developer
5326 - Creative
5325 - Creative
5324 - Creative
5323 - Developer
5322 - Developer
5321 - Developer
5316 - Creative
5315 - Creative
5314 - Creative
5313 - Developer
5312 - Developer
5311 - Developer

52

5266 - Perfectionist*
5265 - Investigator*
5264 - Investigator*
5263 - Achiever
5262 - Achiever
5261 - Achiever
5256 - Perfectionist*
5255 - Investigator*
5254 - Achiever*
5253 - Achiever
5252 - Achiever
5251 - Achiever
5246 - Creative*
5245 - Creative*
5244 - Creative*
5243 - Achiever*
5242 - Achiever*
5241 - Achiever*
5236 - Creative
5235 - Creative
5234 - Creative
5233 - Devoloper
5232 - Developer
5231 - Developer
5226 - Creative
5225 - Creative
5224 - Creative
5223 - Developer
5222 - Developer
5221 - Developer
5216 - Creative
5215 - Creative
5214 - Creative
5213 - Developer
5212 - Developer
5211 - Developer

51

5166 - Perfectionist*
5165 - Investigator*
5164 - Investigator*
5163 - Achiever
5162 - Achiever
5161 - Achiever
5156 - Perfectionist*
5155 - Investigator*
5154 - Investigator*
5153 - Achiever
5152 - Achiever
5151 - Achiever
5146 - Creative*
5145 - Creative*
5144 - Creative*
5143 - Achiever*
5142 - Achiever*
5141 - Achiever*
5136 - Creative
5135 - Creative
5134 - Creative
5133 - Developer
5132 - Developer
5131 - Developer
5126 - Creative
5125 - Creative
5124 - Creative
5123 - Developer
5122 - Developer
5121 - Developer
5116 - Creative
5115 - Creative
5114 - Creative
5113 - Developer
5112 - Developer
5111 - Developer

46

4666 - Practitioner*
4665 - Counselor*
4664 - Counselor*
4663 - Counselor*
4662 - Counselor*
4661 - Counselor*
4656 - Appraiser*
4655 - Appraiser*
4654 - Counselor*
4653 - Counselor*
4652 - Counselor*
4651 - Counselor*
4646 - Appraiser*
4645 - Appraiser*
4644 - Appraiser*
4643 - Counselor*
4642 - Counselor*
4641 - Counselor*
4636 - Appraiser*
4635 - Appraiser*
4634 - Appraiser*
4633 - Persuader
4632 - Persuader
4631 - Persuader
4626 - Appraiser*
4625 - Appraiser*
4624 - Persuader*
4623 - Persuader
4622 - Persuader
4621 - Persuader
4616 - Appraiser*
4615 - Appraiser*
4614 - Persuader*
4613 - Persuader
4612 - Persuader
4611 - Persuader

45

4566 - Practitioner*
4565 - Agent*
4564 - Agent*

4563 - Agent*
4562 - Agent*
4561 - Agent*
4556 - Practitioner*
4555 - Practitioner*
4554 - Practitioner*
4553 - Counselor*
4552 - Counselor*
4551 - Counselor*
4546 - Appraiser*
4545 - Appraiser*
4544 - Appraiser*
4543 - Counselor*
4542 - Counselor*
4541 - Counselor*
4536 - Appraiser*
4535 - Appraiser*
4534 - Appraiser*
4533 - Persuader
4532 - Persuader
4531 - Persuader
4526 - Appraiser*
4525 - Appraiser*
4524 - Appraiser*
4523 - Persuader
4522 - Persuader
4521 - Persuader
4516 - Appraiser*
4515 - Appraiser*
4514 - Appraiser*
4513 - Persuader
4512 - Persuader
4511 - Persuader

44

4466 - Practitioner*
4465 - Agent*
4464 - Agent*
4463 - Agent*
4462 - Agent*
4461 - Agent*
4456 - Practitioner*
4455 - Practitioner*
4454 - Agent*
4453 - Agent*
4452 - Agent*
4451 - Agent*
4446 - Practitioner*
4445 - Practitioner*
4444 - Tight
4443 - Tight
4442 - Inspirational*
4441 - Inspirational*
4436 - Appraiser*
4435 - Appraiser*
4434 - Tight
4433 - Inspirational*
4432 - Inspirational
4431 - Inspirational
4426 - Appraiser*
4425 - Appraiser*
4424 - Appraiser*
4423 - Inspirational
4422 - Inspirational
4421 - Inspirational
4416 - Appraiser*
4415 - Appraiser*
4414 - Appraiser*
4413 - Inspirational
4412 - Inspirational
4411 - Inspirational

43

4366 - Perfectionist*
4365 - Investigator
4364 - Investigator
4363 - Achiever
4362 - Achiever
4361 - Achiever
4356 - Perfectionist*
4355 - Perfectionist*
4354 - Achiever

Biblical Personal Profiles™

4353 - Achiever
4352 - Achiever
4351 - Achiever
4346 - Creative*
4345 - Creative*
4344 - Tight
4343 - Achiever*
4342 - Achiever
4341 - Achiever
4336 - Creative*
4335 - Creative*
4334 - Creative*
4333 - Developer*
4332 - Developer
4331 - Developer
4326 - Creative*
4325 - Creative*
4324 - Creative
4323 - Developer
4322 - Developer
4321 - Developer
4316 - Creative*
4315 - Creative*
4314 - Creative
4313 - Developer
4312 - Developer
4311 - Developer

 42

4266 - Perfectionist*
4265 - Investigator
4264 - Investigator
4263 - Achiever
4262 - Achiever
4261 - Achiever
4256 - Perfectionist*
4255 - Perfectionist*
4254 - Investigator*
4253 - Achiever
4252 - Achiever
4251 - Achiever
4246 - Creative*
4245 - Creative*
4244 - Investigator*
4243 - Achiever
4242 - Achiever
4241 - Achiever
4236 - Creative*
4235 - Creative*
4234 - Creative
4233 - Developer
4232 - Developer
4231 - Developer
4226 - Creative*
4225 - Creative*
4224 - Creative
4223 - Developer
4222 - Developer
4221 - Developer
4216 - Creative*
4215 - Creative*
4214 - Creative
4213 - Developer
4212 - Developer
4211 - Developer

 41

4166 - Perfectionist*
4165 - Investigator
4164 - Investigator
4163 - Achiever
4162 - Achiever
4161 - Achiever
4156 - Perfectionist*
4155 - Perfectionist*
4154 - Investigator
4153 - Achiever
4152 - Achiever
4151 - Achiever
4146 - Creative*
4145 - Creative*
4144 - Investigator*

4143 - Achiever
4142 - Achiever
4141 - Achiever
4136 - Creative*
4135 - Creative*
4134 - Creative
4133 - Developer
4132 - Developer
4131 - Developer
4126 - Creative*
4125 - Creative*
4124 - Creative
4123 - Developer
4122 - Developer
4121 - Developer
4116 - Creative*
4115 - Creative*
4114 - Creative
4113 - Developer
4112 - Developer
4111 - Developer

 36

3666 - Practitioner*
3665 - Counselor*
3664 - Counselor*
3663 - Counselor
3662 - Counselor
3661 - Counselor
3656 - Appraiser*
3655 - Practitioner*
3654 - Counselor*
3653 - Counselor
3652 - Counselor
3651 - Counselor
3646 - Appraiser*
3645 - Appraiser*
3644 - Counselor*
3643 - Counselor
3642 - Counselor
3641 - Counselor
3636 - Appraiser*
3635 - Appraiser
3634 - Appraiser*
3633 - Promoter
3632 - Promoter
3631 - Promoter
3626 - Appraiser*
3625 - Appraiser*
3624 - Appraiser*
3623 - Promoter
3622 - Promoter
3621 - Promoter
3616 - Appraiser*
3615 - Appraiser*
3614 - Appraiser*
3613 - Promoter
3612 - Promoter
3611 - Promoter

 35

3566 - Practitioner*
3565 - Agent*
3564 - Agent*
3563 - Agent
3562 - Agent
3561 - Agent
3556 - Practitioner*
3555 - Practitioner*
3554 - Counselor*
3553 - Counselor
3552 - Counselor
3551 - Counselor
3546 - Appraiser*
3545 - Appraiser*
3544 - Counselor*
3543 - Counselor
3542 - Counselor
3541 - Counselor
3536 - Appraiser*
3535 - Appraiser
3534 - Appraiser*

3533 - Promoter
3532 - Promoter
3531 - Promoter
3526 - Appraiser*
3525 - Appraiser
3524 - Appraiser*
3523 - Promoter
3522 - Promoter
3521 - Promoter
3516 - Appraiser*
3515 - Appraiser
3514 - Appraiser*
3513 - Promoter
3512 - Promoter
3511 - Promoter

 34

3466 - Practitioner*
3465 - Agent*
3464 - Agent*
3463 - Agent
3462 - Agent
3461 - Agent
3456 - Practitioner*
3455 - Practitioner*
3454 - Agent*
3453 - Agent
3452 - Agent
3451 - Agent
3446 - Practitioner*
3445 - Practitioner*
3444 - Practitioner*
3443 - Counselor*
3442 - Counselor*
3441 - Counselor*
3436 - Appraiser*
3435 - Appraiser*
3434 - Appraiser*
3433 - Promoter*
3432 - Promoter*
3431 - Promoter*
3426 - Appraiser*
3425 - Appraiser*
3424 - Appraiser*
3423 - Promoter*
3422 - Promoter
3421 - Promoter
3416 - Appraiser*
3415 - Appraiser*
3414 - Appraiser*
3413 - Promoter*
3412 - Promoter
3411 - Promoter

 33

3366 - Perfectionist
3365 - Perfectionist*
3364 - Specialist*
3363 - Specialist*
3362 - Specialist
3361 - Specialist
3356 - Perfectionist
3355 - Perfectionist*
3354 - Specialist*
3353 - Specialist*
3352 - Specialist
3351 - Specialist
3346 - Objective Thinker*
3345 - Perfectionist*
3344 - Perfectionist*
3343 - Specialist*
3342 - Specialist*
3341 - Specialist*
3336 - Objective Thinker*
3335 - Objective Thinker*
3334 - Objective Thinker*
3333 - Tight
3332 - Tight
3331 - Tight
3326 - Objective Thinker
3325 - Objective Thinker
3324 - Objective Thinker*
3323 - Tight

3322 - Undershift
3321 - Undershift
3316 - Objective Thinker
3315 - Objective Thinker
3314 - Objective Thinker*
3313 - Tight
3312 - Undershift
3311 - Undershift

 32

3266 - Perfectionist
3265 - Investigator*
3264 - Investigator*
3263 - Specialist*
3262 - Specialist
3261 - Specialist
3256 - Perfectionist
3255 - Perfectionist
3254 - Investigator
3253 - Specialist*
3252 - Specialist
3251 - Specialist
3246 - Objective Thinker*
3245 - Perfectionist*
3244 - Perfectionist*
3243 - Investigator*
3242 - Specialist
3241 - Specialist
3236 - Objective Thinker
3235 - Objective Thinker
3234 - Objective Thinker*
3233 - Tight
3232 - Undershift
3231 - Undershift
3226 - Objective Thinker
3225 - Objective Thinker
3224 - Objective Thinker
3223 - Undershift
3222 - Undershift
3221 - Undershift
3216 - Objective Thinker
3215 - Objective Thinker
3214 - Objective Thinker
3213 - Undershift
3212 - Undershift
3211 - Undershift

 31

3166 - Perfectionist*
3165 - Investigator*
3164 - Investigator
3163 - Specialist*
3162 - Specialist
3161 - Specialist
3156 - Perfectionist*
3155 - Perfectionist*
3154 - Investigator
3153 - Specialist*
3152 - Specialist
3151 - Specialist
3146 - Objective Thinker*
3145 - Perfectionist*
3144 - Perfectionist*
3143 - Investigator*
3142 - Specialist
3141 - Specialist
3136 - Objective Thinker
3135 - Objective Thinker
3134 - Objective Thinker*
3133 - Tight
3132 - Undershift
3131 - Undershift
3126 - Objective Thinker
3125 - Objective Thinker
3124 - Objective Thinker
3123 - Undershift
3122 - Undershift
3121 - Undershift
3116 - Objective Thinker
3115 - Objective Thinker
3114 - Objective Thinker
3113 - Undershift

3112 - Undershift
3111 - Undershift

 26

2666 - Practitioner*
2665 - Counselor*
2664 - Counselor*
2663 - Counselor
2662 - Counselor
2661 - Counselor
2656 - Appraiser*
2655 - Practitioner*
2654 - Counselor*
2653 - Counselor
2652 - Counselor
2651 - Counselor
2646 - Appraiser*
2645 - Appraiser*
2644 - Counselor*
2643 - Counselor
2642 - Counselor
2641 - Counselor
2636 - Appraiser*
2635 - Appraiser
2634 - Appraiser*
2633 - Promoter
2632 - Promoter
2631 - Promoter
2626 - Appraiser*
2625 - Appraiser
2624 - Appraiser*
2623 - Promoter
2622 - Promoter
2621 - Promoter
2616 - Appraiser*
2615 - Appraiser
2614 - Appraiser*
2613 - Promoter
2612 - Promoter
2611 - Promoter

 25

2566 - Practitioner*
2565 - Agent*
2564 - Agent*
2563 - Agent
2562 - Agent
2561 - Agent
2556 - Practitioner
2555 - Practitioner*
2554 - Counselor*
2553 - Counselor
2552 - Counselor
2551 - Counselor
2546 - Appraiser*
2545 - Appraiser*
2544 - Counselor*
2543 - Counselor
2542 - Counselor
2541 - Counselor
2536 - Appraiser*
2535 - Appraiser
2534 - Appraiser*
2533 - Promoter
2532 - Promoter
2531 - Promoter
2526 - Appraiser*
2525 - Appraiser
2524 - Appraiser*
2523 - Promoter
2522 - Promoter
2521 - Promoter
2516 - Appraiser*
2515 - Appraiser
2514 - Appraiser*
2513 - Promoter
2512 - Promoter
2511 - Promoter

24

2466 - Practitioner*
2465 - Agent*
2464 - Agent*
2463 - Agent
2462 - Agent
2461 - Agent
2456 - Practitioner*
2455 - Practitioner*
2454 - Agent*
2453 - Agent
2452 - Agent
2451 - Agent
2446 - Practitioner
2445 - Practitioner
2444 - Practitioner*
2443 - Counselor*
2442 - Counselor
2441 - Counselor
2436 - Appraiser*
2435 - Appraiser
2434 - Appraiser*
2433 - Counselor*
2432 - Counselor
2431 - Counselor
2426 - Appraiser*
2425 - Appraiser
2424 - Appraiser
2423 - Promoter
2422 - Promoter
2421 - Promoter
2416 - Appraiser*
2415 - Appraiser
2414 - Appraiser
2413 - Promoter
2412 - Promoter
2411 - Promoter

23

2366 - Perfectionist
2365 - Perfectionist*
2364 - Specialist*
2363 - Specialist
2362 - Specialist
2361 - Specialist
2356 - Perfectionist
2355 - Perfectionist
2354 - Specialist*
2353 - Specialist
2352 - Specialist
2351 - Specialist
2346 - Objective Thinker*
2345 - Perfectionist
2344 - Perfectionist*
2343 - Specialist*
2342 - Specialist
2341 - Specialist
2336 - Objective Thinker
2335 - Objective Thinker
2334 - Objective Thinker*
2333 - Tight
2332 - Undershift
2331 - Undershift
2326 - Objective Thinker
2325 - Objective Thinker
2324 - Objective Thinker
2323 - Undershift
2322 - Undershift
2321 - Undershift
2316 - Objective Thinker
2315 - Objective Thinker
2314 - Objective Thinker
2313 - Undershift
2312 - Undershift
2311 - Undershift

22

2266 - Perfectionist
2265 - Perfectionist*
2264 - Specialist*
2263 - Specialist
2262 - Specialist
2261 - Specialist

2256 - Perfectionist
2255 - Perfectionist
2254 - Specialist*
2253 - Specialist
2252 - Specialist
2251 - Specialist
2246 - Objective Thinker*
2245 - Perfectionist
2244 - Perfectionist
2243 - Specialist
2242 - Specialist
2241 - Specialist
2236 - Objective Thinker
2235 - Objective Thinker
2234 - Objective Thinker
2233 - Undershift
2232 - Undershift
2231 - Undershift
2226 - Objective Thinker
2225 - Objective Thinker
2224 - Objective Thinker
2223 - Undershift
2222 - Undershift
2221 - Undershift
2216 - Objective Thinker
2215 - Objective Thinker
2214 - Objective Thinker
2213 - Undershift
2212 - Undershift
2211 - Undershift

21

2166 - Perfectionist
2165 - Perfectionist*
2164 - Specialist*
2163 - Specialist
2162 - Specialist
2161 - Specialist
2156 - Perfectionist
2155 - Perfectionist
2154 - Specialist*
2153 - Specialist
2152 - Specialist
2151 - Specialist
2146 - Objective Thinker*
2145 - Perfectionist
2144 - Perfectionist
2143 - Specialist
2142 - Specialist
2141 - Specialist
2136 - Objective Thinker
2135 - Objective Thinker
2134 - Objective Thinker
2133 - Undershift
2132 - Undershift
2131 - Undershift
2126 - Objective Thinker
2125 - Objective Thinker
2124 - Objective Thinker
2123 - Undershift
2122 - Undershift
2121 - Undershift
2116 - Objective Thinker
2115 - Objective Thinker
2114 - Objective Thinker
2113 - Undershift
2112 - Undershift
2111 - Undershift

16

1666 - Practitioner*
1665 - Counselor*
1664 - Counselor*
1663 - Counselor
1662 - Counselor
1661 - Counselor
1656 - Appraiser*
1655 - Practitioner*
1654 - Counselor*
1653 - Counselor
1652 - Counselor
1651 - Counselor

1646 - Appraiser*
1645 - Appraiser*
1644 - Counselor*
1643 - Counselor
1642 - Counselor
1641 - Counselor
1636 - Appraiser*
1635 - Appraiser
1634 - Appraiser*
1633 - Promoter
1632 - Promoter
1631 - Promoter
1626 - Appraiser*
1625 - Appraiser
1624 - Appraiser*
1623 - Promoter
1622 - Promoter
1621 - Promoter
1616 - Appraiser*
1615 - Appraiser
1614 - Appraiser*
1613 - Promoter
1612 - Promoter
1611 - Promoter

15

1566 - Practitioner*
1565 - Agent*
1564 - Agent*
1563 - Agent
1562 - Agent
1561 - Agent
1556 - Practitioner
1555 - Practitioner*
1554 - Counselor*
1553 - Counselor
1552 - Counselor
1551 - Counselor
1546 - Appraiser*
1545 - Appraiser*
1544 - Counselor*
1543 - Counselor
1542 - Counselor
1541 - Counselor
1536 - Appraiser*
1535 - Appraiser
1534 - Appraiser*
1533 - Promoter
1532 - Promoter
1531 - Promoter
1526 - Appraiser*
1525 - Appraiser
1524 - Appraiser*
1523 - Promoter
1522 - Promoter
1521 - Promoter
1516 - Appraiser*
1515 - Appraiser
1514 - Appraiser*
1513 - Promoter
1512 - Promoter
1511 - Promoter

14

1466 - Practitioner*
1465 - Agent*
1464 - Agent*
1463 - Agent
1462 - Agent
1461 - Agent
1456 - Practitioner
1455 - Practitioner*
1454 - Agent*
1453 - Agent
1452 - Agent
1451 - Agent
1446 - Practitioner
1445 - Practitioner*
1444 - Practitioner*
1443 - Counselor
1442 - Counselor
1441 - Counselor

1436 - Appraiser*
1435 - Appraiser*
1434 - Appraiser
1433 - Counselor*
1432 - Counselor*
1431 - Counselor*
1426 - Appraiser*
1425 - Appraiser*
1424 - Appraiser
1423 - Promoter
1422 - Promoter
1421 - Promoter
1416 - Appraiser*
1415 - Appraiser*
1414 - Appraiser
1413 - Promoter
1412 - Promoter
1411 - Promoter

13

1366 - Perfectionist
1365 - Perfectionist*
1364 - Specialist*
1363 - Specialist
1362 - Specialist
1361 - Specialist
1356 - Perfectionist
1355 - Perfectionist
1354 - Specialist*
1353 - Specialist
1352 - Specialist
1351 - Specialist
1346 - Objective Thinker*
1345 - Perfectionist
1344 - Perfectionist*
1343 - Specialist*
1342 - Specialist
1341 - Specialist
1336 - Objective Thinker
1335 - Objective Thinker
1334 - Objective Thinker*
1333 - Tight
1332 - Undershift
1331 - Undershift
1326 - Objective Thinker
1325 - Objective Thinker
1324 - Objective Thinker
1323 - Undershift
1322 - Undershift
1321 - Undershift
1316 - Objective Thinker
1315 - Objective Thinker
1314 - Objective Thinker
1313 - Undershift
1312 - Undershift
1311 - Undershift

12

1266 - Perfectionist
1265 - Perfectionist*
1264 - Specialist*
1263 - Specialist
1262 - Specialist
1261 - Specialist
1256 - Perfectionist
1255 - Perfectionist
1254 - Specialist*
1253 - Specialist
1252 - Specialist
1251 - Specialist
1246 - Objective Thinker*
1245 - Perfectionist
1244 - Perfectionist
1243 - Specialist
1242 - Specialist
1241 - Specialist
1236 - Objective Thinker
1235 - Objective Thinker
1234 - Objective Thinker
1233 - Undershift
1232 - Undershift
1231 - Undershift

1226 - Objective Thinker
1225 - Objective Thinker
1224 - Objective Thinker
1223 - Undershift
1222 - Undershift
1221 - Undershift
1216 - Objective Thinker
1215 - Objective Thinker
1214 - Objective Thinker
1213 - Undershift
1212 - Undershift
1211 - Undershift

11

1166 - Perfectionist
1165 - Perfectionist*
1164 - Specialist*
1163 - Specialist
1162 - Specialist
1161 - Specialist
1156 - Perfectionist
1155 - Perfectionist
1154 - Specialist*
1153 - Specialist
1152 - Specialist
1151 - Specialist
1146 - Objective Thinker*
1145 - Perfectionist
1144 - Perfectionist
1143 - Specialist
1142 - Specialist
1141 - Specialist
1136 - Objective Thinker
1135 - Objective Thinker
1134 - Objective Thinker
1133 - Undershift
1132 - Undershift
1131 - Undershift
1126 - Objective Thinker
1125 - Objective Thinker
1124 - Objective Thinker
1123 - Undershift
1122 - Undershift
1121 - Undershift
1116 - Objective Thinker
1115 - Objective Thinker
1114 - Objective Thinker
1113 - Undershift
1112 - Undershift
1111 - Undershift

interpretation stage III:

classical profile pattern interpretations

The interpretations for the *Classical Profile Patterns* are based upon the behavioral tendencies demonstrated by people with specific configurations of plotting points. The positional relationships among the four plotting points could result in hundreds of potential configurations and would require several book length volumes for the interpretations. The Biblical Profile System represents a more pratical approach. The Classical Profile Patterns are those configurations which occur most frequently in a variety of work situations. They represent the *significant* difference in work behavioral styles. Depending upon the degree of difference in the configurations of plotting points, you may have one interpretation for all three graphs or as many as three. The interpretation for each graph should be read from the meaning context of that specificgraph. The following explanation facilitates this process.

GRAPH I: Behavior, Expected by Others

The interpretation for Graph I describes those behavioral tendencies that are most visible to people in your work situation. Based upon the "most" choices, Graph I acknowledges the influence others have on your behavior. This graph reflects the *current* information you are collecting from managers, colleagues, and subordinates about what they expect of you. Graph I is the most dynamic of the three graphs in that it is the most subject to change. Such change is not surprising because the work situation represents our daily "bread and butter."

GRAPH II: Behavior, Instinctive Response to Pressure

The interpretation for Graph II describes those behavioral tendencies that tend to be apparent to others particularly under stress. Graph II reflects the information you have collected from significant persons in the *past*. It contains your history; this is information you have collected, stored, and accepted about yourself. Based upon the "least" choices, this "old" behavior is drawn upon without conscious thought in pressure situations. Graph II tends to be the most static of the graphs. It may change gradually in response to traumatic events that force you to reexamine this information.

GRAPH III: Behavior, Self-Perception

The interpretation for Graph III provides a description of your self-perception. It is a *summary* graph in that it combines the stored and accepted information (Graph II) with the current demands of the present environment (Graph I).

This relationship between the three graphs is depicted in the following figure. It illustrates that, while behavior change can and does occur, the change usually is gradual and in response to the perceived demands of the situation.

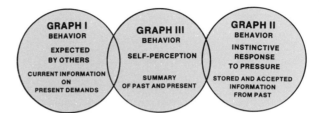

Dissimilar graphs are indicators of change

When Graph I is different from Graph II, you perceive the work environment as demanding work behavioral tendencies that are different from your basic style (Graph II). The difference in the configuration of plotting points may indicate an attempt to develop a new work style in adjusting to the expectations of others. Or the difference between the graphs may indicate specific environmental demands which are causing you stress.

When Graph I is different from Graph II, but similar to Graph III, you have been successful in combining the present demands (Graph I) without altering your history (Graph II) so that you are fairly comfortable with your self-identify (Graph III).

When Graph I is different from Graph III, you may be experiencing a period of growth and some discomfort as you attempt to incorporate new demands (Graph I) with stored information (Graph II). Your behavior may fluctuate during this period of assimilating new behavior.

Similar graphs indicate fewer demands for change

Similarity in the configurations of plotting points on the three graphs indicates that you perceive the work behavioral tendencies demanded by the current work situation (Graph I) as similar to those of past situations (Graph II). Consequently, there is little need to change your self-perception (Group III). This may be due to one or more of the following factors:

1. The work behavioral tendencies demanded by the present work environment *are* similar to those in the past.

2. You control what others can demand of you.

3. The work behavioral tendencies demanded of you are different from those demanded of you in the past, but in lieu of altering your style, you have chosen to *augment*. That is, you have surrounded yourself with people whose work behavioral tendencies complement your style and combine to meet the demands of the situation.

Remove Perforation B to reveal the Classical Profile Pattern interpretations.

Biblical Personal Profiles™

achiever pattern

Martha, Nehemiah

emotions	industrious, diligent; displays frustration
goal	personal accomplishments, sometimes at the expense of group
judges others by	concrete results
influences others by	accountability for own work
value to the organization	sets and completes key result areas for self
overuses	reliance on self; absorption in task
under pressure	becomes frustrated and impatient; may fail to communicate; becomes more of a "doer" and less a "delegator"
fears	others with competing or inferior work standards
would increase effectiveness with more	reduction of "either-or" thinking; clarity of task priority and optional approaches; willingness to compromise short-term for long-range benefits

Achievers are motivated internally and are task oriented. These qualities were found in both Nehemiah and Martha. In Luke 10, Martha was intensely concerned with serving food to Jesus. Nehemiah committed himself to rebuilding the wall around Jerusalem and to reinstituting the Law, two momentous jobs. We see his thorough organizational planning and scheduling go into effect as soon as he had the king's permission for the work. Achievers are practical people who evaluate others by results and can be critical. Martha was clearly indignant that Mary failed to help her serve Jesus. Achievers are indifferent to interference both from people and circumstances. Nehemiah's wall was rebuilt in 52 days despite intense pressure. Achievers hold others accountable to high standards and will take back a delegated task if it is not going satisfactorily. After Nehemiah reinstituted the Covenant and divided responsibilities, he left to report to the king. When he returned and found the people lax, he quickly reestablished control. Achievers need to balance commitment to task with sensitivity to people.

agent pattern

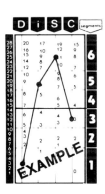

Abraham, Hannah

emotions	accepts affection; rejects aggression
goal	acceptance
judges others by	tolerance and inclusion
influences others by	offering understanding; friendship
value to the organization	supports, harmonizes, empathizes; service oriented
overuses	kindness
under pressure	becomes persuasive through information or key friendships if necessary
fears	dissension; conflict
would increase effectiveness with more	strength in the realization of who they are and what they can do; firmness and self-assertion; would benefit from saying "no" when appropriate

Agents create a supportive, empathetic environment for people as well as for tasks. We see Abraham create such an environment when his servant showed uncertainty in the task of finding a wife for Isaac. Agents' natural ability to listen and to show concern makes them excellent role models for others who want to show understanding and friendship. However, Agents' fear conflict, dissention and confrontation, and this can work against them. We see examples of this when Abraham said that Sarah was his sister in order to avoid conflict and again when he gave in to Sarah's demand that Hagar be removed. Agents normally respond to pressure by internalizing it, which can cause stomach and digestion problems. Hannah encountered this condition until she learned to share the problem with God. When shown love and acceptance, Agents are deeply loyal. Abraham showed this loyalty when he offered God his beloved Isaac. Hannah exhibited her trust when she committed Samuel, her first born, to a life-time service to God. In both, we see God's model of total dedication.

appraiser pattern

David, Miriam (*)

emotions	high drive factor to look good
goal	"win" with flair
judges others by	ability to initiate activities
influences others by	competitive recognition
value to the organization	accomplishes goals through people
overuses	authority or ingenuity
under pressure	becomes restless, critical, impatient
fears	"losing;" looking bad to others
would increase effectiveness with more	individual follow-through; empathy when showing disapproval; pace themselves

Appraisers have an expansive enthusiasm and the ability to inspire others for a cause. Instead of giving orders, they seem to draw people alongside. We see David, an Appraiser, do this when he enlists the aid of his followers in obtaining 200 Philistine foreskins to satisfy the dowry demand for Michal. Appraisers are not intimidated by aggressive people but they reserve admiration for those who show style, charm and flair. David's responsiveness to Abigail is an example of an Appraiser's esteem and appreciation. Appraisers frequently have a bent towards the arts. Both Miriam and David were musicians and performers. Under pressure, Appraisers are very susceptible to temptation and often use their assertiveness to obtain what might be better left alone. We see this when David pursued Bathsheba and then suffered the consequences. In Psalm 32, David shows a Godly sensitivity and a willingness to give his weakness as well as his strength to the Lord's control. In this we see why he is called a man after God's own heart and is mentioned 58 times in the New Testament, including the oft-repeated title given to Jesus--Son of David.

counselor pattern

Abigail, Barnabas

emotions	approachable; affectionate and understanding
goal	friendship; happiness
judges others by	positive acceptance; generally looking for the good in people
influences others by	personal relationships; practicing an "open door" policy
value to the organization	stable, predictable; wide range of friendships; good at listening to feelings
overuses	indirect approach; tolerance
under pressure	becomes overly-flexible and intimate; too trusting without differentiating among people
fears	pressuring people; being accused of causing harm
would increase effectiveness with more	attention to realistic deadlines; initiative in getting the task done

Counselors are approachable, affectionate, understanding people. The Levite Joseph so exemplified these attributes that the Apostles named him Barnabas, Greek for "son of encouragement". Counselors respond readily to the needs of others, such as when Barnabas sold land and placed the money at the Apostles' feet. Alert to others, Counselors frequently put in a good word for an otherwise unnoticed or untried coworker. They are very tolerant, working hard to keep everone happy. Abigail used these skills to convince David not to kill her husband although he was a very crude and evil man. Sometimes this tolerance is a negative trait which we see when Barnabas restricted his fellowhsip with gentiles rather than affront his Jewish friends. Generally, Counselors have an optimistic outlook and see the bright side of people. We see this in Barnabas' good report of Paul, even though the other disciples still feared the ex-Pharisee. Later Barnabas had a similar commitment to John Mark and opposed the strong-minded Paul in this belief. Barnabas and Abigail's unconditional love and belief in people are examples of how important this profile is to the body of Christ.

creative pattern

Paul

emotions	accepts aggression; may be restrained in expression
goal	dominance; unique accomplishments
judges others by	personal standards; progressive ideas in getting the "thing" done
influences others by	setting a pace in developing systems; task or project competition
value to the organization	initiator or designer of changes
overuses	bluntness; critical or condescending attitude
under pressure	easily bored with routine work; sulky when unwillingly restrained; assertive and pioneering
fears	not being influential; failure to achieve their standards
would increase effectiveness with more	warmth; tactful communication; team cooperation; recognition that sanctions exist

Creative patterns are agressive, determined leaders who infuse energy and meaning into lifeless systems. They set the pace in developing new and unusual ideas, usually seeking power and challenges. Paul, a Creative pattern, shows these traits when he preaches that the burden of the Law was replaced by the freedom of grace. His new and untried mission took him to distant lands and people which were sometimes hostile, but Paul persisted and succeeded. Creative persons are detailed and meticulous leaders who are quite blunt and critical. They can be destructive, such as Paul was before his conversion, but can also use their strong characteristics to confront issues that others avoid. We see this in Paul's writings and his frank discussion of the problems among his young churches. When a strong Creative pattern learns to correct others lovingly, such as God helped Paul do through his dealings with Peter, Barnabas, and John Mark, they are a tremendous testimony and building force.

developer pattern

Solomon

emotions	individualistic in the meeting of personal needs
goal	a new opportunity
judges others by	ability to meet the Developer's standards
influences others by	finding solutions to problems; personal sense of power projected
value to the organization	avoids "passing the buck;" new or innovative problem-solving
overuses	control of people and situations to accomplish his/her own results
under pressure	becomes a loner when things need to be done; belligerent if individualism is threatened or doors to challenge are closed
fears	boredom; loss of control
would increase effectiveness with more	patience, empathy; participation and collaboration with others; follow-through and attention to importance of quality control

Developers are strong individuals with high standards. They solve problems alone rather than by consulting associates. In Solomon we see this independent action through his writings: the word "I" is used 41 times in the first two chapters of Ecclesiastes. Developers fear boredom and constantly seek new challenges, a drive which Solomon used to take Israel to its pinnacle of influence. His personal studies and curiosity worked with God's special gift of wisdom to give him unparalled knowledge. Developers sometimes manipulate people and situations in order to get what they want. To build the Temple, Solomon made a covenant with Hiram which he was unable to honor. To gain territories he entered numerous marriage contracts which ultimately caused his downfall and the division of Israel. In his writings, however, Solomon shows us a model of glory and greatness in a Spirit-controlled Developer.

inspirational pattern

D i S C segments

EXAMPLE

Stephen, Laban

emotions	accepts aggression; tends to outwardly downplay their need for affection
goal	controlling their environment or audience
judges others by	how they project personal strength, character and social power
influences others by	charm; direction, intimidation, use of rewards
value to the organization	"people mover;" initiates, demands, compliments, disciplines
overuses	ends justify the means
under pressure	becomes manipulative; quarrelsome; belligerent
fears	being too soft; loss of social status
would increase effectiveness with more	genuine sensitivity; willingness to help others succeed in their personal development separate from him/her where appropriate

Inspirational patterns have strong verbal skills and forceful personalities which can be a mighty combination. Quick in thought and action, Inspirational people welcome confrontations and like to match wits and skills against others. Stephen was known for his eloquent and bold testimony. When he was challenged about his faith, he powerfully refuted the unbelievers and the Sanhedrin in public debates. Because Inspirational people can often identify the motives of another person, they know what others want and will sometimes offer a carrot on a long stick if it serves their purpose. Laban, also an Inspirational profile, changed Jacob's wages ten times in twenty years and gave Leah as a bride when Rachel had been promised. It is important to realize that though Laban and Stephen had the same profile, their value systems toward God differed. Stephen worshipped the living God; Laban respected God but worshipped idols. Stephen exemplifies the Inspirational pattern when totally committed to the will of the Lord.

investigator pattern

D i S C segments

EXAMPLE

Jacob

emotions	dispassionate; self-disciplined
goal	power of formal role positions
judges others by	use of data
influences others by	determination, tenacity
value to the organization	comprehensive, attention to details; working on tasks individually, in dyads, or small groups
overuses	bluntness; suspicion of others
under pressure	tends to internalize conflict; remember wrongs done to them
fears	involvement with the masses; selling abstract ideas
would increase effectiveness with more	flexibility; acceptance of others; personalized involvement

Investigators are steady, determined people who are highly commited to finishing what they start. They break down complex problems and find workable solutions. They are the anchors of reality in an emotional group. Jacob, the Investigator, shows these practical tendencies in everything he sets out to accomplish, including his creation of better breeding methods to increase his herd. Investigators set long range goals and have a tenacious determination to get what they want. Jacob, though constantly manipulated by Laban, persisted in his goal to marry Rachel. He also wrestled with God, clinging to the Almighty unitl he received a blessing. Under pressure, Investigators mentally store grievances which are likely to boil over at some future time. Jacob had such an encounter with Laban and his list was thorough and straightforward. When the encounter was over, however, the air was cleared and the two separated in peace. Jacob, in his steady, behind the scenes way, shows us how God uses this low key pattern to carry through His plan.

objective thinker pattern

D i S C segments

EXAMPLE

Luke, Mary

emotions	tends to reject interpersonal aggression
goal	correctness
judges others by	cognitive ability
influences others by	factual data, logical arguments
value to the organization	defines, clarifies; obtains information; evaluates; tests
overuses	analysis
under pressure	becomes worrisome
fears	irrational acts; ridicule
would increase effectiveness with more	self-disclosure; willingness to experience their real emotional states; sharing their insights and opinions with others in public

Objective thinkers are proper, discrete, and honestly humble. They test and criticize themselves and others, checking and rechecking every aspect of a job. They see beauty in logic. Luke, though not an Apostle, had an intimacy with the Apostles which allowed him to work closely and humbly in recording what they saw and learned. He showed the methodical approach of an Objective pattern in the opening of his gospel: "It seemed fitting for me as well, having investigated everything carefully from the beginning, to write it out for you in consecutive order." Because Objective thinkers internalize information, they tend to play mental gymnastics with their thoughts. Mary, the mother of Jesus, was said to have "kept pondering" on the angel's message concerning the birth of Jesus. Objective thinkers are often extremely shy and self-effacing. Luke, the author of Acts, does not name himself other than by using "we" and "us" when he discussed his travels with Paul. Mary had those same qualities. Both Luke and Mary are gentle, humble people who served the Lord in a quiet support position but whose impact will be felt throughout eternity.

overshift pattern

Segment No. 6555
Pattern: **Overshift**

An overshift occurs when all four plotting points are positioned above the midline (horizontal line 14) on the graph. The person may be experiencing a period of questioning and a lack of self-acceptance. A need to overachieve may be an additional feeling that results in actual overperformance. If the person's work performance is beyond the norm, others in the work environment may comment: "She's quite a worker," or "He's tyring to prove something." The person may inwardly wonder how long the pace can be maintained.

An overshift in Graph 1, **BEHAVIOR, EXPECTED BY OTHERS,** indicates that the person may see the current environment as ambiguous. This ambiguity may be due to insufficient reinforcement for productive behavior or inadequate directions as to expectations. An aid to resolving the overshift is to seek out information regarding expectations.

An overshift in Graph II, **BEHAVIOR, INSTINCTIVE RESPONSE TO PRESSURE,** may indicate that, early in life, the person learned to respond to ambiguous situations with questioning and overachievement.

Further learning may have weakened this behavioral response, but pressure situations tend to uncover this "old" behavior. Eliminating the pressure is a straightforward solution. If this is not possible, awareness of the tendency to this type of response can spur a reexamination of whether this behavior is appropriate to the situation. Another answer is to emulate the behavior of someone who responds well to pressure.

An overshift in Graph III, **BEHAVIOR, SELF-PERCEPTION,** may indicate that the person is experiencing some ambiguity of self-concept, flowing either from a reaction to the current environment or from learned responses in the past. An environment that reinforces current behavior and clarifies expectations helps to resolve the ambiguous work situation.

Note: To determine if the overshift is due to temporary conditions, respond to another Biblical Profile System after a few days. You may also want to request someone who knows you well to take a Biblical Profile System on you. This provides information as to how you are perceived by another person.

---

perfectionist pattern

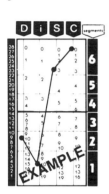

Esther, Moses

emotions	competent in doing things right; restrained; cautious
goal	stable, predictable accomplishments
judges others by	precise standards
influences others by	their demeanor; attention to details and accuracy
value to the organization	conscientious; maintains standards; quality control
overuses	procedures and "failsafe" controls; over dependency on people, products and processes that have worked in past
under pressure	becomes tactful, diplomatic
fears	antagonism
would increase effectiveness with more	role flexibility; independence and interdependence; belief in self as a worthwhile person in their own right

Perfectionists work at setting and maintaining high standards. It is important to them that things are done correctly and they will often establish quality control systems. They pay meticulous attention to details. Moses, the Perfectionist, communicated God's Law and recorded a wealth of historical data without embellishment. Typically, Perfectionists internalize instructions by asking questions before they act in their methodical and orderly manner. They often need concrete personal reassurance before moving ahead. At the burning bush, Moses asked God five questions. Still, Moses hesitated. God then gave him additional support in Aaron. After reflecting, he went. Although restrained and cautious, once Perfectionists are committed to a plan they remain loyal to the end. Moses and Esther were willing to sacrifice their lives for the Jewish people. Moses is remembered as the only person to whom God spoke face-to-face. Esther's unselfish actions saved God's people and made the Feast of Purim possible.

---

persuader pattern

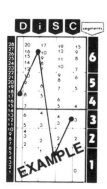

Peter, Rebekah

emotions	trusts others; enthusiastic
goal	authority and prestige; a variety of status symbols
judges others by	ability to verablize; flexibility
influences others by	friendly manner; openness; verbal adeptness
value to the organization	seller, closer; delegates responsibility; poised, confident
overuses	enthusiasm, oversells, optimism
under pressure	becomes soft and persuadable; organized when desires to look good
fears	a fixed environment; complex relationships
would increase effectiveness with more	challenging assignments; attention to task-directed service and key details; objective analysis of data; collective perspective

Persuaders are skilled orators, responding quickly and convincingly in any situation. It was Peter who fervently proclaimed to Jesus, "Thou art the Christ, the Son of the Living God." Persuaders inspire others, a trait God used when Peter was chosen to lead the Apostles. Persuaders are also closers; they don't fear asking for the order. Peter became a great evangelist not only because of his inspired, impromptu sermons but because he had the natural boldness to ask for a decision. Persuaders thrive on people, variety, and mobility. Rebekah's eager willingness to marry a man she had not seen even though her family had reservations shows this trait. In the case of Peter, we see him constantly interacting with people and traveling throughout Israel, Syria and Rome. Persuaders are often too optimistic about themselves and oversell their abilities. Peter confidently proclaimed he would never deny Jesus but did so that very night. Yet after Pentecost, Peter became poised and grounded in Jesus Christ. His boldness before the Sanhedrin in Acts 4 shows how God can change a Persuader from vacilating Simon into Peter, the rock.

practitioner pattern

Elijah

emotions	feels able to match or surpass others in effort and technical performance
goal	high personal ambitions
judges others by	self-discipline; their position and advancements
influences others by	confidence in ability to enlarge skills; developing and following "proper" procedures and actions
value to the organization	skilled in technical and people problem solving; proficient in specialty
overuses	manipulation to promote themselves; unrealistic expectations of others
under pressure	becomes restrained; sensitive to criticism
fears	being too predictable; being unrecognized
would increase effectiveness with more	appreciation of others; genuine collaboration for common benefit; delegation of key tasks to appropriate individuals

Practitioners have an intensity for life and strive for excellence, especially in their chosen field. They are competent, capable people with high ambitions and self-disciplined sufficiency. Elijah, a Practitioner, constantly fought both the religious and secular systems of his day, striving to gain recognition for the God of Israel. Practitioners are amiable, but when they think something is not being done right they can become caustic. They like things done the right way, their way, and create procedures to reach their goals. Elijah showed this when he set up a test to determine which prophets truly represented God. When Baal did not respond, Elijah mocked Jezebel's prophets, then used his authority to cast sentence on them. Like most Practitioners, Elijah was sensitive to criticism and susceptible to depression. When Jezebel vowed to kill him, Elijah fled and prayed that God would take his life. In God's response we see how love can encourage a Practitioner from depths of despair to service.

promoter pattern

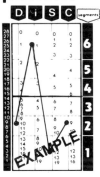

Aaron, Saul

emotions	willing to accept others
goal	approval, popularity
judges others by	verbalization skills
influences others by	praises, opportunities, favors
value to the organization	relieves tension; promotes projects and people, including themselves
overuses	praise, optimism
under pressure	becomes careless and sentimental; disorganized in getting "things" done
fears	loss of social acceptance and self-worth
would increase effectiveness with more	control of time, objectivity; sense of urgency; emotional control; follow-through on promises, tasks

Promoters are articulate communicators with strong interpersonal skills. They are eager and skilled in promoting people and projects. Aaron, a Promoter, was selected to communicate God's plan to Pharaoh and to represent the Israelite's cause when Moses complained that he was slow of speech. When Promoters are under pressure, they become careless and disorganized. Saul, also a Promoter, shows this characteristic looseness when he resorted to situational ethics and personally offered burnt offerings. Promoters dread the loss of social recognition. Although Saul had lost God's blessing, he convinced Samuel to walk with him before the elders and people. Exodus 32 shows that Aaron, like Saul, was unable to withstand social pressures. However, Aaron later recognized his sin and repented, something that Saul was unwilling to do. He was then able to promote God's holy name among his people as the first High Priest.

result-oriented pattern

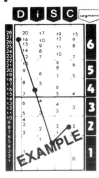

Joshua, Sarah

emotions	high verbalized ego strength; displays rugged individualism
goal	dominance and independence
judges others by	ability to accomplish the task quickly
influences others by	force of character; persistence
value to the organization	"show 'em" attitude and actions
overuses	impatience, win-lose competition
under pressure	becomes critical and fault-finding; resists participating in a team; may overstep prerogatives
fears	others will take advantage of them; slowness, especially in task activities; being too 'soft' or 'close' with others
would increase effectiveness with more	verbalization of his reasoning; seeking other views and ideas about his goals, in solving problems; genuine concern for others; patience and humility

Result Oriented people persevere when antagonistic circumstances make others falter. Joshua believed Canaan was conquerable, but the majority ruled against him. As a result, the Israelites wandered for 39 years. People of this profile are often trailblazers and leaders, as we see after Moses' death when Joshua was put in charge and he led the people into the promised land. Joshua also exemplified the Result Oriented pattern's tendency to take command. The word command, or commanded, is used 49 times in the book of Joshua, frequently by Joshua himself as he gave instructions. People with this profile can influence others by sheer force of character and personality, qualities which help them lead but can make them overbearing. Among their greatest need is to balance drive of character with patience and humility. Sarah's plan to gain an heir through Abraham and Hagar shows this strength in need of balance. Later she would truly learn humility by her loving submission to Abraham, who was the weaker of the two personalities. God helped Joshua develop patience by placing him under Moses' humble but Godly leadership.

specialist pattern

Issac

emotions	calculated moderation, accommodating
goal	status quo; controlled environment
judges others by	friendship standards; then competency
influences others by	consistency of performance; accommodation
value to the organization	short-term planner; predictable, consistent; maintains steady pace
overuses	modesty; low risk-taking; passively resistant to innovation
under pressure	becomes adaptable to those in authority and group-thinking
fears	change, disorganization
would increase effectiveness with more	sharing of their ideas; self-confidence based on feedback; short-cut methods; focus on critical tasks and details

Specialists are consistent people who "wear well" and work to maintain the status quo. In Isaac, God confirmed the Abrahamic Covenant and Isaac worked well within this established plan. Specialists are tolerant and accomodating as we see in Isaac's relations with the Philistines. Under pressure, Specialists will avoid conflict at any price such as when Isaac encountered trouble and moved on rather than fight. However, when God told him not to go to Egypt, he obeyed. Specialists do not enjoy confrontation and Isaac, like his father, said that his wife was his sister rather than face conflicts. Emotionally, Specialists are middle of the road. The most extreme behavior we see in Isaac is his grief over Esau's marriage to heathens and his violent trembling when he gave Esau's birthright to Jacob. Both cases involve family disorganization which is a key fear of the Specialist. Specialists are faithful, but without a lot of fanfare. We see this in Isaac as he faithfully committed himself to his father's God and thus becomes known as a patriarch of God's chosen people.

tight pattern

Segment No. 4444
Pattern: **Tight**

A tight configuration occurs when all four plotting points are clustered in the same segment of the graph. The clustering indicates that the person may be trying to be all things to all people. For example, the desire to make quick decisions may be counterbalanced by an equal attempt to work with and through people. In addition, the person may be attempting to accomplish all of the work while also trying to ensure the quality. Behavior may alternate between periods of furious activity and periods of overwhelmed frustration.

A tight configuration in Graph I, **BEHAVIOR, EXPECTED BY OTHERS,** may indicate that the person is receiving insufficient reinforcement for productive behavior or inadequate direction concerning priorities in the work environment. Clarifying what others expect in the work situation may help to resolve the attempt to be all things to all people.

A tight configuration in Graph II, **BEHAVIOR, INSTINCTIVE RESPONSE TO PRESSURE,** may indicate that the person, early in life, learned to respond to an ambiguous situation by trying to please everyone. The results were cycles of frustration alternating with great effort. Later learning may

have lessened this behavioral response, but pressure situations tend to unearth this "old" behavior. Eliminating the pressure is a straightforward solution. If this is not possible, awareness of the tendency toward the response can spur a reexamination of whether this behavior is appropriate to the current work situation. Another answer is to emulate the behavior of someone who responds well to pressure.

A tight configuration in Graph III, **BEHAVIOR, SELF-PERCEPTION,** may indicate that the person is experiencing some ambiguity about self, flowing either from the present environment or from past experiences. Reinforcement of productive behavior and clarification of expectations tend to resolve a tight configuration.

Note: To determine if the tight configuration is due to temporary conditions, respond to another Biblical Profile System in a few days. You may also wnat to request someone who knows you well to take a Biblical Profile System on you. This provides information as to how you are perceived by another person.

undershift pattern

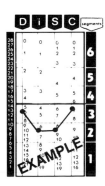

Segment No. 3223
Pattern: **Undershift**

An undershift occurs when all four plotting points are positioned below the midline (horizontal line 14) on the graph. The person may be experiencing a period of discouragement and a lack of self-acceptance. Feelings of underachieving or an actual drop in work performance may be additional factors. If there is a drop in performance, the person may be subject to some criticism. Even if performance is maintained, the individual may have self-doubts. Comments from others in the work environment may range from "He's just never satisfied with what he does," to "She's really not doing very well."

An undershift in Graph I, **BEHAVIOR, EXPECTED BY OTHERS,** may indicate that the person perceives the work environment as ambiguous. This ambiguity may be due to insufficient reinforcement for productive behavior or inadequate directions as to what is expected. Clarifying the expectations of others may help to resolve the undershift.

An undershift in Graph II, **BEHAVIOR, INSTINCTIVE RESPONSE TO PRESSURE,** may indicate that, early in life, the person learned to respond to ambiguous

situations with feelings of discouragement. Further learning may have weakened this behavioral response, but pressure situations tend to unearth this "old" behavior. Eliminating the pressure is a straightforward solution. If this is not possible, awareness of the tendency to this type of responsecan spur an analysis of whether this behavior is appropriate to the situation.

An undershift in Graph III, **BEHAVIOR, SELF-PERCEPTION,** may indicate that the person is experiencing some uncertainty of self-identity, flowing either from a reaction to the current environment or from learned responses in the past. An environment that reinforces productive behavior and clarifies expectations helps to resolve the ambiguous situation.

Note: To determine if the undershift is due to temporary conditions, respond to another Biblical Profile System after a few days. You may also want to request someone who knows you well to take a Biblical Profile System on you. This provides information as to how you are perceived by another person.

Biblical Personal Profiles™

DiSC™ Profile and Scripture Parallels

DiSC™ CLASSICAL PATTERNS[1]	POSITIVE BIBLICAL ROLE MODELS	SCRIPTURE REFERENCE
Achiever Pattern	Martha (*), Nehemiah	Luke 10:38-42; Nehemiah 2,3
Agent Pattern	Abraham, Hannah	Gen. 24,21; I Sam. 1,2
Appraiser Pattern	David, Miriam (*)	I Sam. 18, 16, 21; Ex. 15:20-21
Counselor Pattern	Abigail, Barnabas	I Sam. 25; Acts4:36-37;9:26-27
Creative Pattern	Michal (*), Paul	II Sam. 6:14-23; Gal. 2; Acts 15
Developer Pattern	Lydia (*), Solomon	Acts 16:13-15, 40 Eccl. 2; I Kings 9:10-28
Inspirational Pattern	Apollos, Laban Stephen	Acts 18:24-28; Gen. 29:15-30 Acts 6, 7
Investigator Pattern	Anna (*), Jacob James	Luke 2:36-38; Gen. 29, 30, 31, 32; Acts 15-13-21
Objective Thinker Pattern	Luke, Mary, Ruth	Luke 1:1-4; Luke 1:26-56 Ruth 2:2, 10; 3:1-18
Perfectionist Pattern	Esther, John Moses	Esther 4; John 19:26-27 Exodus 3, 4, 20, 32
Persuader Pattern	Peter, Rebekah	Matt. 16, 26; Acts 3; Gen. 24
Practitioner Pattern	Deborah (*), Elijah, Jonah	Judges 4, 5; I Kings 18,19; Jonah 4
Promoter Pattern	Aaron, King Saul	Exodus 4:14-17, 32:1-6; I Sam. 15
Result-Oriented Pattern	Joshua, Sarah (*)	Joshua 1; Gen. 16; I Peter 3:6
Specialist Pattern	Dorcas (*), Issac	Acts 9:36-38; Gen. 26, 27

In associating a *Classical Pattern* with a person from Scripture, a detailed study was done of the specific behavior of individuals in the Bible. When a character exhibited consistent tendencies of the *Classical Pattern*, the name was listed as model for that pattern. In some cases, the tendencies indicate a specific pattern but not enough information was recorded in Scripture to make a confident association. Those people are indicated by (*).

The Greek words "Choleric", "Sanguine", "Phlegmatic", and "Melancholic" are similar terms to the DiSC™ used by some Christian writers to identify differences in behavior. Most known is Dr. Tim LaHaye. In addition, Gary Smalley and John Trent use animal figures to represent four personality styles: Lion (D), Otter (I), Golden Retriever (S) and Beaver (C). Carlson Learning Company has not reviewed the validity of these instruments, nor their interpretative materials.

A common inquriy to the profiles of Biblical characters is, "What was Jesus' profile?" A resource dealing with this issue is **Understanding Jesus, A Personality Profile** by Ken Voges (Moody Press, 1992) which analyzes the personality traits of Jesus through the template of the **Biblical Personal Profiles** intensity index. Available through your Performax or Family Discovery Distributor.

The association of the *Classical Patterns* with persons in Scripture and case studies are the discernment of the author and In His Grace, Inc., and do not necessarily represent the opinions of Carlson Learning Company.

[1]John G. Geier, Dorothy E. Downey, **Library of Classical Profile Patterns,** Carlson Learning Company, January, 1979.

DiSC™ Environments
How to be more effective with people of different DiSC™ tendencies

HIGH D (PAUL)
CASE STUDY: ACTS 9:3-19

Remember a High D May Want:

Authority, challenges, prestige, freedom, varied activities, difficult assignments, logical approach, opportunity for advancement.

HOW TO RESPOND TO THE HIGH D

- Provide direct answers, be brief and to the point; confrontation may be necessary to gain their attention.
- Ask "what" questions, not how.
- Stick to business.
- Outline possibilities for person to get results, solve problems, be in charge.
- Stress logic of ideas or approaches.
- When in agreement agree with facts and idea, not person.
- If timelines or sanctions exist get them into open but relate them to end results or goal.

HIGH i (PETER)
CASE STUDY: JOHN 21:1-22

Remember a High i May Want:

Social Recognition, popularity, people to talk to, freedom of speech, freedom from control and detail, recognition of abilities, opportunities to help and motivate others.

HOW TO RESPOND TO THE HIGH i

- Provide favorable friendly environment; never use confrontation if you want productive feedback.
- Allow them to express their intuition and ideas.
- Provide ideas for transferring talk to action.
- Provide testimonials of experts on ideas.
- Allow time for stimulating and fun activities.
- Provide details in writing but don't dwell on them.
- Create a democratic environment.
- Provide incentives for taking on tasks.

HIGH C (MOSES)
CASE STUDY: EXODUS 3-4

Remember a High C May Want:

Security, no sudden changes, personal attention, little responsibility, exact job descriptions, controlled work environment, status quo, reassurance, to be part of a group.

HOW TO RESPOND TO THE HIGH C

- Prepare your case in advance.
- Provide straight pros and cons of ideas.
- Support ideas with accurate data.
- Provide reassurances that no surprises will occur.
- Provide exact job description with precise explanation of how it fits in the big picture.
- Provide step by step approach to a goal.
- If agreeing be specific.
- If disagreeing, disagree with the facts, not the person; strongly reject "poor-me" comments.
- Provide many explanations in a patient and persistent manner.

HIGH S (ABRAHAM)
CASE STUDY: GENESIS 12-22

Remember a High S May Want:

Status quo, security of situation, time to adjust, appreciation, identification with group, work pattern, limited territory, areas of specialization.

HOW TO RESPOND TO THE HIGH S

- Provide a sincere, personal and agreeable environment.
- Show a sincere interest in the person.
- Ask "how" questions to get an opinion. Allow for and use visual illustrations.
- Be patient in drawing out their goals.
- Present ideas or departures from status quo in a non-threatening manner; give them a chance to adjust.
- Define their roles or goals in the plan.
- Provide personal assurances of support.
- Emphasize how their actions will minimize their risk.

Biblical Personal Profiles™

Biblical Personal Profiles™

"Love Your Neighbor as yourself." Scripture commands it but how can I obey it? Does love mean putting up with his bad habits? What about the things she does that really need changing?

The *Biblical Personal Profiles*™ answer these questions as it gives you insight and understanding into your spouse, your neighbor and yourself. by matching the DiSC™ Classical Patterns (of human behavior) with illustrations from the Bible, you see how God used, changed, encouraged and admonished people just like you, your spouse and your friends.

The *Biblical Personal Profile*™ has been used in classrooms, counseling sessions, retreats and seminars. It is a simple instrument designed to give you an eye opening view of why people do as they do. It is a tool that will help you love, accept and encourage the people in your life.

Biblical Personal Profiles™
Published by Carlson Learning Company, Minneapolis, MN, U.S.A.
In association with In His Grace, Inc., Houston, TX, U.S.A.

Dimensions of Behavior

BIBLICAL PERSONAL PROFILES

A VALUABLE INSIGHT INTO SCRIPTURAL CHARACTERS

By Ken Voges

Carlson Learning Company

IN ASSOCIATION WITH IN HIS GRACE, INC.

NAME _____ DATE _____

*Additional sheets of response forms and instructions for a second respondent
are included in this *Biblical Personal Profile.*

Choose *one* MOST and *one* LEAST in each of the 24 groups of words.

	MOST	LEAST		MOST	LEAST		MOST	LEAST		MOST	LEAST
1 gentle	◯	◯	**7** fussy	◯	◯	**13** aggressive	◯	◯	**19** respectful	◯	◯
persuasive	◯	◯	obedient	◯	◯	extroverted	◯	◯	pioneering	◯	◯
humble	◯	◯	unconquerable	◯	◯	amiable	◯	◯	optimistic	◯	◯
original	◯	◯	playful	◯	◯	fearful	◯	◯	accommodating	◯	◯
2 attractive	◯	◯	**8** brave	◯	◯	**14** cautious	◯	◯	**20** argumentative	◯	◯
introspective	◯	◯	inspiring	◯	◯	determined	◯	◯	adaptable	◯	◯
stubborn	◯	◯	submissive	◯	◯	convincing	◯	◯	nonchalant	◯	◯
sweet	◯	◯	timid	◯	◯	good-natured	◯	◯	light-hearted	◯	◯
3 easily led	◯	◯	**9** sociable	◯	◯	**15** willing	◯	◯	**21** trusting	◯	◯
bold	◯	◯	patient	◯	◯	eager	◯	◯	contented	◯	◯
loyal	◯	◯	self-reliant	◯	◯	agreeable	◯	◯	positive	◯	◯
charming	◯	◯	soft-spoken	◯	◯	high-spirited	◯	◯	peaceful	◯	◯
4 open-minded	◯	◯	**10** adventurous	◯	◯	**16** confident	◯	◯	**22** good mixer	◯	◯
obliging	◯	◯	receptive	◯	◯	sympathetic	◯	◯	cultured	◯	◯
will power	◯	◯	cordial	◯	◯	tolerant	◯	◯	vigorous	◯	◯
cheerful	◯	◯	moderate	◯	◯	assertive	◯	◯	lenient	◯	◯
5 jovial	◯	◯	**11** talkative	◯	◯	**17** well-disciplined	◯	◯	**23** companionable	◯	◯
precise	◯	◯	controlled	◯	◯	generous	◯	◯	accurate	◯	◯
nervy	◯	◯	conventional	◯	◯	animated	◯	◯	outspoken	◯	◯
even-tempered	◯	◯	decisive	◯	◯	persistent	◯	◯	restrained	◯	◯
6 competitive	◯	◯	**12** polished	◯	◯	**18** admirable	◯	◯	**24** restless	◯	◯
considerate	◯	◯	daring	◯	◯	kind	◯	◯	neighborly	◯	◯
joyful	◯	◯	diplomatic	◯	◯	resigned	◯	◯	popular	◯	◯
harmonious	◯	◯	satisfied	◯	◯	force of character	◯	◯	devout	◯	◯

*Descriptive root words adapted from *Emotions of Normal People* by William Moulton Marsten

instructions

1. responding

1. Study the first group of words on page 2 while thinking about the behavioral tendencies you show in a specific setting or focus.
   (MY SPECIFIC FOCUS IS:_____)

2. Select only one word that **MOST** describes you. Use a coin to rub over the oval after that word in the **MOST** column. A symbol will appear. See EXAMPLE 1.

3. Select *only* one word that **LEAST** describes you. Use a coin to rub over the oval after the word in the **LEAST** column. A symbol will appear.

4. Use the Same procedure to respond to the remaining groups of descriptive words.
   Remember: *Only* one **MOST** and one **LEAST** choice for each group.

EXAMPLE 1

This individual tends to be most original and least gentle in the selected setting.

	MOST	LEAST
1. gentle	⬭	▲
persuasive	⬭	⬭
humble	⬭	⬭
original	N	⬭

2. counting and recording

1. Tear out the perforated area in the lower right of this page to reveal the tally box.

2. *Most Choices:*
   Total the number of Z's in the four **MOST** columns on page 2. Write this total over the Z symbol in the **MOST** column of the tally box.

   Use the same procedure to count and record the other symbols ■ ▲ ★ N in the **MOST** columns.

3. *Least Choices:*
   Total the number of Z's in the four **LEAST** columns on page 2. Write this total over the Z symbol in the **LEAST** column of the tally box.

   Use the same procedure to count and record the other symbols ■ ▲ ★ N in the **LEAST** columns.

4. Check the accuracy by adding the **MOST** and **LEAST** columns of the tally box. Each column should total 24.

3. determining the difference

1. Determine the difference between the **MOST** and **LEAST** columns for each row of the tally box. Enter these numbers in the **DIFFERENCE** column. See EXAMPLE 2.

2. Use a plus (✚) sign if the number in the **MOST** column is greater than the number in the **LEAST** column. See example.

   Use a minus (▬) sign if the number in the **MOST** column is less than the number in the **LEAST** column.

EXAMPLE 2

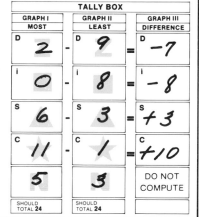

TALLY BOX		
GRAPH I MOST	**GRAPH II** LEAST	**GRAPH III** DIFFERENCE
D 2	D 9	D −7
i 0	i 8	i −8
s 6	s 3	s +3
c 11	c ★	c +10
5	3	DO NOT COMPUTE
SHOULD TOTAL **24**	SHOULD TOTAL **24**	

PERFORATION A PERFORATION A PERFORATION A PERFORATION

LIFT AND TEAR PERFORATION "A" TO REVEAL

TALLY BOX

Biblical Personal Profiles™

instructions
plotting

4.

1. Use the numbers from the **MOST** column of the tally box to plot Graph I. See example 3.

   Plot the **Z** number on the **D** line. ──────

   Plot the **■** number on the **i** line. ──────

   Plot the **▲** number on the **S** line. ──────

   Plot the **★** number on the **C** line. ──────

   Estimate the plotting point if a specific number is not shown on the graph. The "N" number was used to ensure accurate results and is not plotted.

2. Use the numbers from the **LEAST** column of the tally box to plot Graph II.

3. Use the numbers from the **DIFFERENCE** column of the tally box to plot Graph III. Note the + and — signs on **Graph III**.

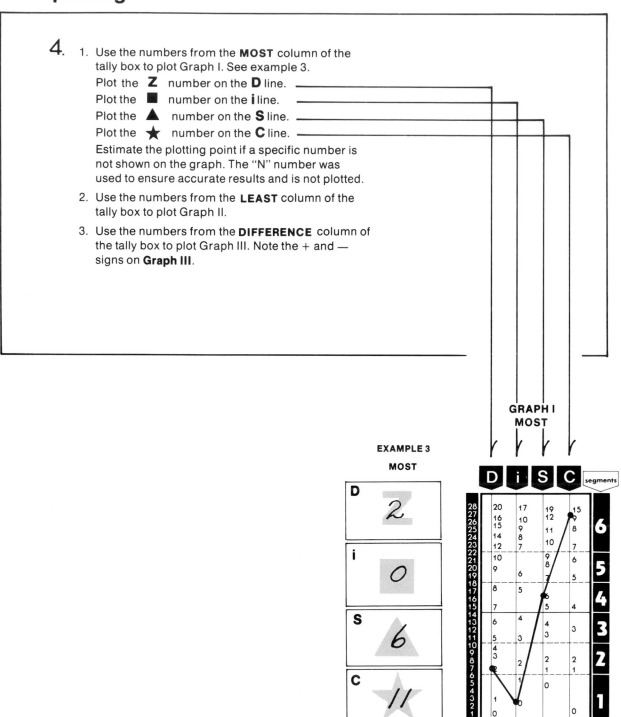

GRAPH I
MOST

EXAMPLE 3

MOST

Biblical Personal Profiles™

140

GRAPH I behavior:
expected by others

MOST

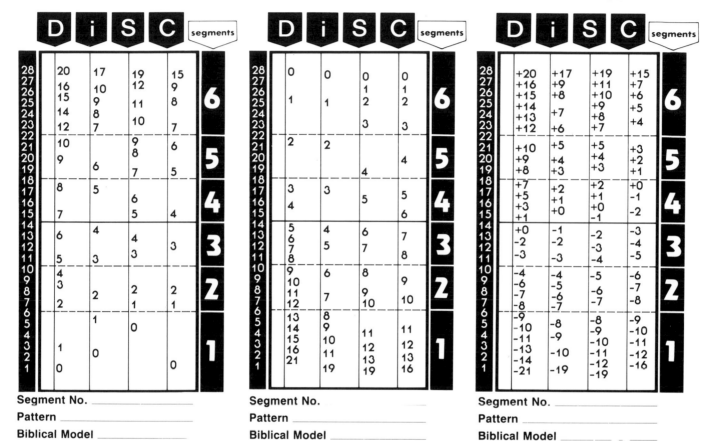

	D	i	S	C	segments
28	20	17	19	15	
27	16	10	12	9	
26	15	9		8	
25	14	8	11		**6**
24	12	7	10	7	
23					
22	10		9	6	
21	9		8		
20		6		5	**5**
19			7		
18	8	5			
17			6		
16	7		5	4	**4**
15					
14	6	4	4		
13				3	
12	5	3	3		**3**
11					
10	4				
9	3		2	2	
8		2	1	1	**2**
7	2				
6		1	0		
5					
4	1				
3		0			**1**
2					
1	0			0	

Segment No. _____

Pattern _____

Biblical Model _____

GRAPH II behavior:
instinctive response to pressure

LEAST

	D	i	S	C	segments
28	0	0	0	0	
27					
26			1	1	
25	1	1	2	2	**6**
24					
23			3	3	
22					
21	2	2			
20				4	**5**
19			4		
18					
17	3	3		5	
16	4		5		**4**
15				6	
14	5	4	6	7	
13	6				
12	7	5	7	8	**3**
11	8				
10	9	6	8	9	
9	10				
8	11	7	9	10	**2**
7	12		10		
6	13	8			
5	14	9	11	11	
4	15	10	12	12	
3	16	11	13	13	**1**
2	21				
1		19	19	16	

Segment No. _____

Pattern _____

Biblical Model _____

GRAPH III behavior:
self-perception

DIFFERENCE

	D	i	S	C	segments
28	+20	+17	+19	+15	
27	+16	+9	+11	+7	
26	+15	+8	+10	+6	
25	+14		+9	+5	**6**
24	+13	+7	+8		
23	+12	+6	+7	+4	
22					
21	+10	+5	+5	+3	
20	+9	+4	+4	+2	**5**
19	+8	+3	+3	+1	
18					
17	+7	+2	+2	+0	
16	+5	+1	+1	-1	**4**
15	+3	+0	+0	-2	
14	+1		-1		
13	+0	-1	-2	-3	
12	-2	-2	-3	-4	**3**
11	-3	-3	-4	-5	
10					
9	-4	-4	-5	-6	
8	-6	-5	-6	-7	**2**
7	-7	-6	-7	-8	
6	-8	-7			
5	-9	-8	-8	-9	
4	-10	-9	-9	-10	
3	-11		-10	-11	
2	-13	-10	-11	-12	**1**
1	-14	-19	-12	-16	
	-21		-19		

Segment No. _____

Pattern _____

Biblical Model _____

---

1. Circle the peak of the four plotting points in Graph I. See **Example 4**

2. Use Graph II if you have two equal high points in Graph I.

3. Identify the scale for that plotting point. The example shows a high point on the **S** scale.

4. Turn to page 6.

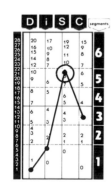

Example 4

Completed by _____

Specific Focus _____

Date _____

TALLY BOX		
GRAPH I **MOST**	**GRAPH II** **LEAST**	**GRAPH III** **DIFFERENCE**
D	− D	= D
i	− i	= i
S	− S	= S
C	− C	= C
N	N	DO NOT COMPUTE
SHOULD TOTAL **24**	SHOULD TOTAL **24**	

interpretation
stage I:
general highlights

1. Read the section on **D, i, S** or **C** which correspond(s) to the scale of your highest plotting point(s) on Graph I and Graph II. Refer to Page 13 for more information about the meaning of each Graph to help you decide which is more significant for you at this time.

2. Personalize this *general* interpretation by:
   - Underlining the phrases which describe you accurately
   - Deleting the phrases which do not apply to you
   - Substituting appropriate phrases from the other descriptions

3. Read the other sections to appreciate the general differences in **D, i, S** and **C** behavioral tendencies.

D dominance

EMPHASIS IS ON SHAPING THE ENVIRONMENT BY OVERCOMING OPPOSITION TO ACCOMPLISH RESULTS

DESCRIPTION

This person's tendencies include:
- getting immediate results
- causing action
- accepting challenges
- making quick decisions
- questioning the status quo
- taking authority
- managing trouble
- solving problems

This person desires an environment which includes:
- power and authority
- prestige and challenge
- opportunity for individual accomplishments
- wide scope of operations
- direct answers
- opportunity for advancement
- freedom from controls and supervision
- many new and varied activities

ACTION PLAN

This person needs others who:
- weigh pros and cons
- calculate risks
- use caution
- structure a more predictable environment
- research facts
- deliberate before deciding
- recognize the needs of others

To be more effective, this person needs:
- difficult assignments
- understanding that they need people
- techniques based on practical experience
- an occasional shock
- identification with a group
- to verbalize the reasons for conclusions
- an awareness of existing sanctions
- to pace self and to relax more

---

i influencing of others

EMPHASIS IS ON SHAPING THE ENVIRONMENT BY BRINGING OTHERS INTO ALLIANCE TO ACCOMPLISH RESULTS

DESCRIPTION

This person's tendencies include:
- contacting people
- making a favorable impression
- verbalizing with articulateness
- creating a motivational environment
- generating enthusiasm
- entertaining people
- desiring to help others
- participating in a group

This person desires an environment which includes:
- popularity, social recognition
- public recognition of ability
- freedom of expression
- group activities outside of the job
- democratic relationships
- freedom from control and detail
- opportunity to verbalize proposals
- coaching and counseling skills
- favorable working conditions

ACTION PLAN

This person needs others who:
- concentrate on the task
- seek facts
- speak directly
- respect sincerity
- develop systematic approaches
- prefer dealing with things to dealing with people
- take a logical approach
- demonstrate individual follow-through

To be more effective, this person needs:
- control of time, if **D** or **S** is below the midline
- objectivity in decision-making
- participatory management
- more realistic appraisals of others
- priorities and deadlines
- to be more firm with others if **D** is below the midline

C cautiousness/compliance (to their standards)

EMPHASIS IS ON WORKING WITH EXISTING CIRCUMSTANCES TO PROMOTE QUALITY IN PRODUCTS OR SERVICE

DESCRIPTION

This person's tendencies include:
- attention to key directives and standards
- concentrating on key details
- working under known controlled circumstances
- being diplomatic with people
- checking for accuracy
- critical thinking
- critical of performance
- complying with authority

This person desires an environment which includes:
- security assurances
- standard operating procedures
- sheltered environment
- reassurance
- no sudden or abrupt changes
- being part of a work group
- personal responsiveness to their effort
- status quo unless assured of quality control
- door openers who call attention to accomplishments

ACTION PLAN

This person needs others who:
- desire to expand authority
- delegate important tasks
- make quick decisions
- use policies only as guidelines
- compromise with the opposition
- state unpopular positions

To be more effective, this person needs:
- precision work
- opportunity for careful planning
- exact job and objective descriptions
- scheduled performance appraisals
- as much respect for people's personal worth as for what they accomplish
- to develop tolerance for conflict

S steadiness

EMPHASIS IS ON COOPERATING WITH OTHERS TO CARRY OUT THE TASK

DESCRIPTION

This person's tendencies include:
- performing an accepted work pattern
- sitting or staying in one place
- demonstrating patience
- developing specialized skills
- concentrating on the task
- showing loyalty
- being a good listener
- calming excited people

This person desires an environment which includes:
- security of the situation
- status quo unless given reasons for change
- minimal work infringement on home life
- credit for work accomplished
- limited territory
- sincere appreciation
- identification with a group
- traditional procedures

ACTION PLAN

This person needs others who:
- react quickly to unexpected change
- stretch toward the challenges of an accepted task
- become involved in more than one thing
- are self-promoting
- apply pressure on others
- work comfortably in an unpredictable environment
- delegate to others
- are flexible in work procedures
- can contribute to the work

To be more effective, this person needs:
- conditioning prior to change
- validation of self-worth
- information on how one's efforts contribute to the total effort
- work associates of similar competence and sincerity
- guidelines for accomplishing the task
- encouragement of creativity
- confidence in the ability of others

---

interpretation stage II:
dimensional intensity index

The second stage of interpretation considers each dimension separately. The index reflects the intensity of your tendencies on the **D**, **i**, **S**, and **C** scales. To reveal your emerging behavioral pattern, use the following procedure:

1. Draw a horizontal line from the **D** plotting point to a number in the shaded bar at the left of Graph II on page 5. See **Example 5**.

2. Use the indentified number from the shaded bar to locate the corresponding number in the shaded bar of the **D** column *on this page*.

3. Use a coin to rub the space following the number. (A word will appear.)

4. Rub the three spaces below and the three spaces above this reference point. For example, if the number in the shaded bar is 5, color in 2, 3, 4, 5, 6, 7, and 8 for a total of seven spaces.

5. Follow the above procedure for the **i**, **S**, and **C** plotting points.

6. Develop **Graphs II** and **III**, if the configurations are different from **Graph I**, to reveal changes in your pattern under those conditions.

7. Personalize your interpretation:
   • Use an **x** to indicate agreement
   • Use an **O** to indicate disgreement
   • Use a **?** to indicate doubt

Example 5

D		i		S		C	
28		28		28		28	
27		27		27		27	
26		26		26		26	
25		25		25		25	
24		24		24		24	
23		23		23		23	
22		22		22		22	
21		21		21		21	
20		20		20		20	
19		19		19		19	
18		18		18		18	
17		17		17		17	
16		16		16		16	
15		15		15		15	
14		14		14		14	
13		13		13		13	
12		12		12		12	
11		11		11		11	
10		10		10		10	
9		9		9		9	
8		8		8		8	
7		7		7		7	
6		6		6		6	
5		5		5		5	
4		4		4		4	
3		3		3		3	
2		2		2		2	
1		1		1		1	

Moody Press, a ministry of the Moody Bible Institute, is designed for education, evangelization, and edification. If we may assist you in knowing more about Christ and the Christian life, please write us without obligation: Moody Press, c/o MLM, Chicago, Illinois 60610.